BRINGING BACK OUR
OCEANS

BY CAROL HAND

CONTENT CONSULTANT

Ellen K. Pikitch
Professor and Executive Director
Institute for Ocean Conservation Science
Stony Brook University School of Marine
and Atmospheric Sciences

Essential Library
An Imprint of Abdo Publishing
abdopublishing.com

CONSERVATION
SUCCESS STORIES

abdopublishing.com

Published by Abdo Publishing, a division of ABDO, PO Box 398166, Minneapolis, Minnesota 55439. Copyright © 2018 by Abdo Consulting Group, Inc. International copyrights reserved in all countries. No part of this book may be reproduced in any form without written permission from the publisher. Essential Library™ is a trademark and logo of Abdo Publishing.

Printed in the United States of America, North Mankato, Minnesota
092017
012018

THIS BOOK CONTAINS
RECYCLED MATERIALS

Cover Photo: Rich Carey/Shutterstock Images
Interior Photos: US Fish and Wildlife Service, 4–5; Ted Mclaren/ZumaPress/Newscom, 6–7; Shutterstock Images, 9, 17, 35, 37, 52; K. Jorgen/iStockphoto, 10–11; Kleber Cordeiro/Shutterstock Images, 12; Brendan Delzin/Shutterstock Images, 14; Lynn Seeden/iStockphoto, 18, 98 (bottom); Patrick Endres/Newscom, 20–21, 98 (top); NOAA Photo Library, 24–25; K. Cline/iStockphoto, 26; Olivier Hertel/Sipa USA/AP Images, 28; Jeff Rotman/Science Source, 30; Robert F. Bukaty/AP Images, 32; Andrew J. Martinez/Science Source, 38–39; D. P. Wilson/FLPA/Science Source, 41; Mark Conlin/VWPics/AP Images, 42, 98 (middle left); Alan Hagman/Los Angeles Times/Getty Images, 44, 98 (middle right); NA Image/Shutterstock Images, 45; Richard B. Levine/Newscom, 48; Erich Schlegel/ZumaPress/Newscom, 49; Flip Nicklin/Minden Pictures/Newscom, 51; The Nature Conservancy, 55; Rainer von Brandis/iStockphoto, 56–57; John Anderson Photo/iStockphoto, 60, 99 (top); Yvette Cardozo/Alamy, 61; Rainer Lesniewski/Shutterstock Images, 63; iStockphoto, 64, 94; Shafiqul Alam/Corbis/Getty Images, 66–67; The Ocean Cleanup/Cover Images/Newscom, 72; Hannah McKay/Reuters/Newscom, 73; David Parsons/iStockphoto, 74; Neil Burton/Shutterstock Images, 77; Michel Euler/AP Images, 79; Brian Lasenby/Shutterstock Images, 82–83, 99 (bottom); Davor Lovincic/iStockphoto, 84; Malte Christians/picture-alliance/dpa/AP Images, 86; Red Line Editorial, 93; Rosanne Tackaberry/Alamy, 97

Editor: Marie Pearson
Series Designer: Laura Polzin

Publisher's Cataloging-in-Publication Data

Names: Hand, Carol, author.
Title: Bringing back our oceans / by Carol Hand.
Description: Minneapolis, Minnesota : Abdo Publishing, 2018. | Series: Conservation success stories | Includes online resources and index.
Identifiers: LCCN 2017946784 | ISBN 9781532113154 (lib.bdg.) | ISBN 9781532152030 (ebook)
Subjects: LCSH: Marine resources conservation--Juvenile literature. | Restoration ecology--Juvenile literature. | Conservation of natural resources--Juvenile literature.
Classification: DDC 333.9164--dc23
LC record available at https://lccn.loc.gov/2017946784

CONTENTS

Green sea turtles nest in more than 80 countries.

SEA TURTLES: AN EARLY WARNING

Every year, visitors to the southern coast of Florida might get lucky. At night between May and October, they might see big, clumsy, green sea turtles lumbering out of the water and onto the beach. The turtles are an impressive sight, with shells averaging 4.9 feet (1.5 m) long. The top shell, or carapace, is black on babies but changes color throughout life. It eventually becomes shades of gray, green, brown, or black, forming starburst or irregular patterns. Every two to four years, turtles mate offshore, and the mothers swim to the beach, where they build deep nest cavities above the high tide line. They lay an average of 136 eggs. During a season, they might repeat this process two or three times, laying more eggs every 12 to 14 days.[1]

Scientists have monitored a 13-mile (21 km) stretch of beach in southern Florida's Archie Carr National Wildlife Refuge since the 1980s. In the early days, they counted fewer than 50 green sea turtle nests per year. In 2015, they counted a record 12,026 nests. According to Kate Mansfield, assistant professor at the University of Central Florida, "It is a really remarkable recovery and reflects a 'perfect storm' of conservation successes."[2] Why were there so few nests in the 1980s, and what caused the impressive recovery of Florida's green sea turtles?

Volunteers use dark, red lights to monitor green sea turtles at night. These lights don't disrupt the turtles' nesting habits as much as white light does.

LIGHT UP THE NETS!

In Magdalena Bay, off Mexico's Baja California, gillnet fishing threatens loggerhead turtles. John Wang of the University of Hawaii suggested putting lights on gillnets. When the lights hit the water, they turn on, warning turtles about the net. When the lights come out of the water, they turn off. The lights have reduced the number of turtles caught in nets at night by 40 percent.[3] Some fishers have even reported an increase in fish caught when using the lights.

SAVING THE GREEN SEA TURTLE

In 1978, green sea turtles were classified as endangered under the US Endangered Species Act. This gave them special protection in the United States. Two agencies oversee their protection. The US Fish and Wildlife Service (USFWS) protects their beach nesting grounds. The National Oceanic and Atmospheric Administration (NOAA) protects them in the ocean. This includes both their coastal feeding grounds, such as seagrass beds, and the open ocean, where turtles often become entangled in fishing nets.

The green sea turtle is one of the largest of the seven sea turtle species. Its populations around the world have declined significantly because of human activity. People wait for turtle mothers to come ashore and lay their eggs. Then they kill the mother and raid the nests, obtaining both meat and eggs. Coastal development destroys beaches. Vehicle traffic on beaches discourages mother turtles from nesting, and artificial lights disorient hatchlings trying to reach the ocean. Turtles' seagrass feeding grounds are threatened by pollution and loose soil settling over the beds and killing the plants. In the open ocean, fishermen accidentally kill many sea turtles. They are caught in shrimp trawlnets or gillnets, or they are hooked on longlines. Many of them drown. These hazards threaten not just green sea turtles but all sea turtle species.

USFWS programs work to limit the impact of development and artificial lighting on nesting sites. They establish federal refuges (such as the Archie Carr Refuge) where turtles can nest undisturbed. NOAA now requires all shrimp trawlers to use a special technology: Turtle Excluder Devices (TEDs). TEDs decrease the number of turtles caught in nets because the nets' design allows turtles to escape from the nets. But US government agencies don't save green turtles by themselves. This turtle is one of the world's most protected species. Other countries have passed laws to protect them. The International Union for the Conservation of Nature and Natural Resources (IUCN) has listed them as endangered. Trade in turtle meat and shells is banned by the Convention on International Trade in Endangered Species of Wild Flora and Fauna.

Many universities and research organizations, including Mote Marine Laboratory and the National Marine Life Center, research and restore sea turtle populations. Private organizations such as the

THE IUCN CLASSIFIES SEA TURTLES

The IUCN keeps a red list that classifies major species according to how threatened they are. A critically endangered species is the most likely of the categories to become extinct in the wild. An endangered species faces a great risk of extinction, and a vulnerable species is at a slightly lower risk than an endangered one. IUCN has classified the seven sea turtle species as follows:

Leatherback: Vulnerable
Green: Endangered
Loggerhead: Endangered
Hawksbill (pictured): Critically Endangered
Olive Ridley: Vulnerable
Kemp's Ridley: Critically Endangered
Flatback: Not Enough Information

Sea Turtle Conservancy and Oceana work to protect sea turtles. Also, sea turtles have captured the public's imagination, and people want to protect them. They see photos of turtles entangled in fishing nets. People on the beach may encounter them laying eggs. Several organizations sponsor volunteer groups that patrol beaches, band turtles for satellite tracking, and otherwise protect and study them. Green turtles are still at risk in many places. But at the Archie Carr National Wildlife Refuge, and other areas with active protection, they are a major success story.

Of the sea turtles that hatch on the southeastern coast of the United States, only approximately 1 in 1,000 to 1 in 10,000 survive to adulthood.[4]

SEA TURTLE LIFE AND HAZARDS

Sea turtles begin as tiny, clumsy babies, clawing their way out of eggs and tumbling over one another in their sand dune nests. They race, covered with

Temperature can determine the gender of sea turtle hatchlings. Warmer temperatures produce more female hatchlings.

SAVING BABY TURTLES

On the Caribbean island of Utila in 2014, 150 volunteers from the conservation organization Sea Shepherd patrolled the beaches. Patrols kept poachers away from hawksbill turtle nests so poachers could not steal the eggs or kill the mothers for their meat and shells. Volunteers hid the nests, covered turtle tracks, and coordinated with the island's police. Thanks to their efforts, all turtle moms returned safely to the ocean. Approximately 3,600 hawksbill hatchlings made it successfully to the ocean.[6] Hawksbills are still critically endangered, but volunteers may help them survive.

sand, toward the ocean. If they are very lucky, they avoid predators such as seabirds and raccoons and enter the water. There, many succumb to other predators, including fish. Surviving sea turtles migrate long distances through the open ocean between feeding and nesting grounds. One leatherback turtle, fitted with a tracking device, traveled 12,000 miles (19,300 km) between Indonesia and Oregon. Turtles spend years in the ocean, some living as long as 70 to 80 years. But, when it comes time for reproduction, every mother turtle returns to the very beach on which she hatched. This takes from 5 to 35 years, depending on the species.[5]

Sea turtles roam the world ocean and face a long list of dangers. On beaches, killing for food and the destruction of nesting grounds are still serious threats. There is also a flourishing illegal trade in turtle shells. Beautifully patterned hawksbill shells are particularly desired for jewelry making. Coastal development, such as seawalls, alters or destroys nesting sites.

Sea turtles are built for swimming, but they encounter dangers in the ocean. They must breathe air, and they cannot withdraw their heads and flippers into their shells, making them vulnerable to boats and fishing gear. Hundreds of thousands of turtles die every year from entrapment in fishing gear. Ocean plastics are no less deadly. When leatherback turtles see floating plastic bags, they mistake them for jellyfish, their main food source. Many choke on the bags or starve as bags fill their stomachs. All sea turtles may become entangled in ocean debris. Sea turtles—like other ocean organisms—are vulnerable to the global threats of toxic ocean pollution and climate change.

TOUR DE TURTLES

Since 2008, the Sea Turtle Conservancy has sponsored an event called Tour de Turtles: A Sea Turtle Migration Marathon. The group fits turtles of four species with satellite tracking monitors and tracks them online to show their migration path and the distance they travel. The winner is the turtle that travels the greatest distance. In 2016, 14 turtles competed. The winner, Lady Aurelia, swam 3,465 miles (5,576 km).[7] The Tour de Turtles increases awareness of sea turtle species and the threats they face. Each turtle is assigned a particular cause, such as oil spills, and the public supports their favorite turtle through online donations.

Projects to save sea turtles vary, concentrating on different hazards and different parts of turtle life cycles. The Billion Baby Turtles project, run by the organization SEE Turtles, raises funds from individuals, schools, businesses, and sea turtle tours. They help protect baby sea turtles throughout Latin America. They pay local residents to patrol nesting beaches and protect the mother turtles and their eggs. Other projects, such as those run by the World Wildlife Fund (WWF), involve working with communities or promoting use of new technology, including turtle-friendly hooks, TEDs, and satellite trackers.

Leatherbacks travel farther between breeding and feeding than any other sea turtle species.

WHY SEA TURTLES MATTER

Each sea turtle species plays its own valuable role in maintaining ocean ecosystems. Green turtles, the only herbivorous sea turtle, maintain seagrass beds and nearby coral reefs. Like mowing a lawn, their grazing keeps the beds healthy; their waste returns nutrients to the ecosystem. Seagrass beds support fish and invertebrates and serve as nurseries for their young. Thus, green turtles indirectly maintain many ocean species. Hawksbill turtles feed on sponges, providing more space for corals to grow and thereby increasing coral reef diversity. Leatherbacks feed on jellyfish and help control their populations. As leatherback populations decline, jellyfish populations rise. Jellyfish outcompete fish species, upsetting ocean food webs.

> "We can share the beaches and ocean with sea turtles, but it requires commitment and effort on our part. We can make certain that future generations will have the opportunity to know these unusual animals."[8]
>
> —*Victoria B. Van Meter,* Florida's Sea Turtles

Perhaps even more importantly, what happens to sea turtles happens to the ocean as a whole. Sea turtles face specific threats, but most human activities that threaten them also threaten other ocean species. During their life cycles, sea turtles visit or live in most types of ocean habitats—both in the open ocean and near shore. This small group of species illustrates the range of conservation practices necessary to save the ocean. Turtle survival depends on the health and integrity of the entire ocean, as well as the goodwill of humans. Saving sea turtles will help save the ocean—and vice versa.

NOT JUST ONE ECOSYSTEM

The ocean makes up 99 percent of the space on Earth where plants and animals live.[9] Sea surface temperatures vary greatly from the poles to the equator. Climates are typically divided into three zones: tropical, temperate, and polar. Tropical regions, nearest the equator, are warmest and receive the most precipitation. Temperate zones, in the midlatitudes, have moderate temperatures and year-round rainfall. Polar regions are at the highest latitudes. Temperatures are usually below freezing, and precipitation is low. Large chunks and sheets of ice float in the polar seas.

The ocean is also divided into four zones based on depth and distance from land. The intertidal zone is where ocean meets land. It may be submerged or exposed, depending on tides. In the pelagic zone, organisms float or swim. Much of this is open ocean. The benthic zone is the ocean bottom, where animal life feeds primarily on plant or animal particles and bacteria. The benthic zone drops off into the very deep abyssal zone.

Light, temperature, and pressure vary by ocean depth. Sunlight penetrates only the top layer of water to approximately 660 feet (200 m).[10] Blue light penetrates the farthest, giving the ocean its color. Below this, the ocean becomes inky black.

Temperature also decreases with depth. Surface temperatures are warm in the tropics, moderate in temperate zones, and cold at the poles. At the poles, the cold goes all the way to the ocean floor. Elsewhere, there is a boundary layer, called the thermocline, where temperature changes very rapidly. Below the thermocline, the water remains between 32 and 37.5 degrees Fahrenheit (0 and 3°C).[11] It does not freeze because the salt in ocean water lowers its freezing point to 28.5 degrees Fahrenheit (-1.9°C).[12]

Intertidal Zone

Pelagic Zone

Benthic Zone

Abyssal Zone

The ocean's zones are home to many different species.

Picking up trash on beaches prevents it from ending up in the ocean and harming wildlife.

TWO

THE SCOPE OF MARINE CONSERVATION

Marine, or ocean, conservation is the protection and maintenance of ocean organisms and ecosystems. Marine conservation includes either setting up areas where organisms can live undisturbed or leaving previously disturbed areas alone so organisms and ecosystems can recover. This is the recovery, or "let nature take its course," approach. Marine conservation also includes human intervention to actively restore already damaged ecosystems, which is the process

of restoration ecology. Finally, it includes mitigation, or the slowing or stopping of human activities that damage marine ecosystems. Marine conservation biology is the application of the science of biology to marine conservation.

Sometimes, marine conservationists focus on saving individual species, such as sea turtles, whales, seals, or polar bears. These animals capture people's attention and generate sympathy. It is easier to raise money to save baby seals than to save their polar ecosystems. But without healthy ecosystems, a wide variety of species will not survive. So, although baby seals may seem a lot more cuddly than their ecosystems, saving entire ecosystems is vital.

WHAT THREATENS THE OCEAN?

Of course, people must recognize ocean threats before they can stop the threats. They must be able to restore habitats before irreparable damage

One threat to the ocean is overfishing, which occurs when so many fish are caught that the fish left in the ocean cannot maintain population numbers.

happens. And the ocean faces many threats. Historically, people thought they could exploit ocean resources without limits and dump trash and pollutants into the ocean without consequences. Now, as people see the results of such actions, they are beginning to realize the ocean is more fragile than once thought. Humans have abused it, and it is deteriorating.

One of the largest threats to the ocean is unsustainable fishing. Some fish and shellfish species are deliberately harvested, while others are killed as bycatch during fishing. This has led to the depletion of many marine species. Even though the ocean covers most of the planet, only approximately 3.4 percent of the ocean surface is protected in marine parks or reserves.[1]

Most ocean threats begin at the shore. Some stem from coastal development. Others result from dumping pollutants, including raw sewage, fertilizers, pesticides, toxic chemicals, oil, and plastics. Offshore oil and gas exploration impacts marine species through drilling and oil spills. Coastal oil refineries spill their pollution into coastal waters. Coastal marine habitats such as coral reefs and seagrass beds are the first to be damaged by threats from shore. Open ocean feels the damage, too. Ship anchors cause benthic damage and pollution at ports, and they dump oil and garbage at sea.

BECOMING A MARINE CONSERVATIONIST

Dr. Lance Morgan is president of Marine Conservation Institute. Dr. Morgan advises prospective marine conservationists to get an undergraduate degree in the area that most excites them (from biology to computer science to photography). Morgan also has a master's degree in marine science and a PhD in ecology. He considers hands-on experience vital for marine conservationists. This might include volunteering as an intern or as a field or research assistant. During his career, Dr. Morgan has worked with orcas and deep-sea corals. He worked for California's Marine Mammal Center and NOAA's National Marine Fisheries Service. He also worked at the undersea Aquarius Habitat off Key Largo, Florida.

WHY CARE ABOUT THE OCEAN?

Those living in landlocked areas may wonder why they should care about the ocean. But the ocean has an impact on the entire atmosphere and on the global water cycle. Tiny ocean phytoplankton produce more than half of the oxygen we breathe.[2] The hydrologic cycle transports water around Earth. Water evaporates from the ocean surface, winds move it around Earth, and it precipitates as rain or snow. The ocean is Earth's life-support system.

WHY THE OCEAN IS IMPORTANT

The Woods Hole Oceanographic Institution gathered statistics to illustrate how vital the ocean is to life on Earth:

- The ocean provides 50 percent of the oxygen produced by photosynthesis.
- The ocean holds 90 percent of the heat made by global warming.
- Ocean ships carry 90 percent of international trade.
- People have yet to explore 95 percent of the ocean.[3]

The ocean also supports life by maintaining Earth's temperature. It absorbs much of the excess carbon dioxide produced by human activities. Some carbon dioxide is used by phytoplankton in photosynthesis, and some dissolves in the water. Earth's air temperatures are currently rising, but without ocean carbon dioxide absorption, temperatures would be far higher. Ocean carbon dioxide absorption, plus the movement of heat around Earth by ocean currents, controls climate and temperature and reduces the impacts of climate change throughout Earth.

In addition, ocean fisheries provide one-sixth of the protein consumed by humans. Ocean organisms are a continuing source of new medicines. Ocean shipping routes move almost all goods produced for human use across the ocean. The ocean is essential to human life, health, and economy, as well as weather and climate.

WORKING TO SAVE THE OCEAN

Marine conservation agencies within the US government oversee the country's major ocean resources. The Office of Marine Conservation (OMC) in the State Department makes and implements US policy on international issues relating to living marine resources, including fisheries and aquaculture. NOAA Fisheries protects marine mammals and endangered marine life. It enforces two US laws: the Endangered Species Act and the Marine Mammal Protection Act. NOAA Fisheries protects animals such as whales, corals, sea turtles, and salmon, while still allowing people to use the ocean for fishing, recreation, and other economic activities.

Some marine conservation organizations, such as the Marine Conservation Institute, have a general focus. Others, such as Sea Turtle Conservancy or Coral Reef Alliance, focus on a specific marine organism or ecosystem. These groups take on a variety of different

NOAA conducts research on marine species including orcas.

PEOPLE CAN HELP SAVE THE OCEAN

Everything that becomes trash or pollution can eventually end up in the ocean, and everyone's lifestyle influences the ocean, regardless of where they live. Individuals can cut down on trash and pollution and save the ocean by limiting fertilizer use to decrease excess nutrients that cause algal blooms. They can buy pesticide-free food and avoid using pesticides or toxic cleaning products that can end up in the ocean. They can use reusable grocery bags, cups, and containers to limit plastic pollution. They can also participate in beach cleanups to limit the trash entering the ocean, buy sustainably harvested seafood, and avoid buying souvenirs made from marine organisms (especially coral).

activities, including fund-raising, beach cleanup, educational projects, ecosystem restoration, and technology development. For example, Greenpeace is committed to establishing more marine reserves so 20 percent of US waters are protected by 2020.[4] The group feels this is necessary to end unsustainable fishing and preserve ocean biodiversity. Some Greenpeace activists even engage in acts of civil disobedience, such as boarding oil drilling rigs without permission to protest Arctic oil drilling.

KEEPING IT POSITIVE

In 2009, two researchers at Yale University, Holly Jones and Oswald Schmitz, were concerned that recent reports in ecology were too bleak and despairing. The reports suggested that humans were causing damage to ecosystems that was either irreparable or would take generations to repair. Jones and Schmitz reviewed ecosystem studies done over the past 100 years to determine how long it actually takes damaged ecosystems to recover. They found good news: most ecosystems can recover in a generation or less, if the source of damage is removed and restoration is done. The ocean recovers faster than land. Marine benthic ecosystems, for example, recover in approximately ten years. "The message of our paper," the authors say, "is that recovery is possible and can be rapid for many ecosystems, giving much hope for humankind to transition to sustainable management of global ecosystems."[5]

People need this hope. Science writers such as Rachel Dearborn interpret the condition of the ocean for the public. Dearborn says it is easy to feel engulfed in "a culture of doom and gloom."[6] Unless scientists can offer some success stories, the public may feel hopeless and give up, rather than work to save the ocean. Dr. Nancy Knowlton of the Smithsonian Institution is dedicated to sharing success stories of ocean conservation. She points out that medical professionals don't talk about only medical problems; they also talk about solutions and successes. She thinks the difference may be that, with the ocean, "success is hard to define, complex to prove and impossible to guarantee in the long-term."[7] But on the Smithsonian's Ocean Portal website, a new section called #OceanOptimism is sharing successes and urging individuals to add their own examples.

"No matter where you live, the ocean affects your life."[8]

—*Woods Hole Oceanographic Institution*

In 2017, Monaco launched the *Yersin*, which houses researchers while they are studying biodiversity and how climate change affects the ocean.

Ocean successes are large and small. They range from restoring oyster reefs in Chesapeake Bay to weaving carpets from discarded fishing nets in the Philippines. They are done by volunteers, nonprofit organizations, governments, and intergovernmental groups. No success by itself is enough. But, hopefully, all the large and small successes added together can save the world ocean.

"I look at marine conservation biologists as akin to the doctors of the ocean. And doctors don't train just to write obituaries. They fill medical journals with stories of advances and successes."[9]

—*Dr. Nancy Knowlton,*
Smithsonian Institution

Fisheries observers travel on commercial fishing boats and track information about the fish caught to help protect fish populations.

Chapter
THREE

SAVING OCEAN FISHERIES

Georges Bank is at the southwestern end of the Grand Banks, a series of plateaus on the North American continental shelf. It reaches from Newfoundland in Canada to southern New England. A bank is a huge shoal, or underwater plateau submerged in shallow water. In 2010, the haddock population of Georges Bank underwent a "baby boom." That year, approximately 500 million baby haddock hatched—the most fishers had seen in more than 30 years. Haddock take several years to reach harvest size. This means a boom supplies fisheries for several years. The amount of adult fish large enough to be caught on Georges Bank was approximately 202,384 short tons (183,600 metric tons) in 2013. This represents

Fishing in Georges Bank disturbs the seabed. This makes it harder for some marine species to survive.

a major success for the Georges Bank haddock population, which had crashed in the mid-1990s. Numbers have been increasing since the early 2000s. According to Fisheries and Oceans Canada, estimated haddock levels in 2014 were the highest since 1970.[1]

HADDOCK RECOVERY

Georges Bank is larger than the state of Massachusetts. Many important fish and shellfish breed and feed there, including haddock, cod, flounder, herring, lobster, scallops, and clams. Many have been overfished. Haddock numbers were so low in 1994 that officials closed the fishery from 1995 until 2004. This decade was the longest time since 1900 that the fishery had not been heavily overfished.

The haddock recovery has been most dramatic because of occasional boom years. Cod recover more slowly because their reproduction remains slow and steady. Sea scallops are also increasing—a good sign for the ecosystem, since scallops are immobile. Unlike fish, scallops cannot swim away from unfavorable conditions; thus, their population increase suggests a healthy environment. Luke Gaulton of Fisheries and Oceans Canada attributes the increasing populations to favorable environmental conditions, lower fishing pressure, and a decline in the capture of small fish. Fish populations increase when small fish remain in the population to grow and reproduce. While the haddock were recovering their populations, scientists and government agencies worked with the fishers. Since fishers' livelihoods depend on how many fish they catch, they are often more concerned with maximizing their present-day catch than with future catches. Experts hope to encourage fishers to focus more on long-term fishing strategies to make the fishery more sustainable.

THE DECLINE OF OCEAN FISHERIES

Between 1950 and 2003, the ocean's large fish populations declined by 90 percent.[2] This included

STOPPING SEAFOOD FRAUD

Seafood fraud is the illegal practice of misleading consumers about seafood to increase profits for the sellers. In 2015, the United States began a seafood traceability program. It traces seafood from the time it is caught until it reaches the consumer. Federal, state, or local authorities collect information at ports and enter it into a central database for tracking. Data collected include the seafood's origin, who caught it, when it was caught, and what gear was used. NOAA hopes this will limit illegal fishing and make it easier to enforce catch limits.

open ocean fish, such as tuna, swordfish, and marlin. It also included benthic species, also called groundfish, such as the cod, halibut, and flounder found in shallow areas including the Grand Banks. The main culprit in these drastic fish declines was the rise of technology in the fishery industry. Increases in the sizes of ships and fleets, highly mechanized fishing gear, and floating factories that allowed fish to be immediately preserved all led to dramatic rises in fish catches. Marine biologist Sylvia Earle thinks two other factors have hastened the declines. First, human demand for seafood is increasing. Data support her contention: people in 2012 ate four times as much fish as in 1950.[3] Second, governments spend billions of dollars subsidizing fisheries, trying to sustain jobs and a way of life. But if fish populations cannot replenish themselves after fishing, they are doomed anyway. Researchers say habitat destruction, pollution, climate change, and invasive species also contribute to fish declines, but it is difficult to determine the exact impact of each factor.

"Whereas longlines used to catch ten fish per a hundred hooks, now they are lucky to catch one."[4]

—Ransom Myers, Dalhousie University, on Japanese open-ocean fishing, 2003

Many fisheries scientists have trouble accepting the drastic decline in fish stocks. This may be because they compare the most recent data only with data from the years immediately prior. They have forgotten or never knew the huge sizes that fish attained in the past. The largest individuals have been caught, and recent fishing has been so intense that fish in the 2010s never reach great sizes. According to fisheries biologist Ransom Myers, today's remaining blue marlin reach only one-fifth of their average weight in the past.[5]

Fishing pressure is so high that fish are caught when they are small, often before they can reproduce.

SAVING OCEAN FISHERIES WITH A SINGLE ACT

Whatever the cause of ocean fisheries' decline, saving them is a huge task. It often boils down to large-scale governmental and economic actions. One example is the 1976 Magnuson-Stevens Fishery Conservation and Management Act. The act has two major purposes: to end overfishing and to rebuild depleted fish populations. Both involve preventing fishers from taking more fish in a year than the population can replace. The act sets guidelines for limiting the amount of fish that can be harvested by foreign countries, negotiating treaties on fishery conservation and management, developing conservation plans, and banning destructive fishing practices.

The Magnuson-Stevens Act has benefited many species. When the Georges Bank fisheries for cod, flounder, and haddock were closed, New England sea scallops benefited, too. Their populations were fully

RETURN OF THE CLAMS

The Great South Bay off Long Island, New York, produced more than one-half of all US clams until overfishing destroyed the population. In 2004, the Nature Conservancy bought 13,400 acres (5,400 ha) of the Great South Bay. Working with local communities, it began to restore the clam population. The organization bought clams that were headed to market, and it relocated three million of them into 50 acres (20 ha) of the submerged land, where the clams reproduced. By 2009, 5,000 acres (2,000 ha) had reached the target clam density. Approximately 320 million baby clams had settled either on Conservancy land or adjacent land.[6] This represented a big success for Great South Bay clams.

restored by 2001, and these sea scallops now belong to the world's most valuable wild sea scallop fishery. Mid-Atlantic bluefish populations had plummeted by the late 1990s. A nine-year recovery program was so successful that bluefish were declared fully recovered by 2009, a year ahead of schedule. The Pacific lingcod was also very depleted. A ten-year recovery program rebuilt its population several years ahead of schedule.

"Rebuilding our ocean fisheries makes good environmental and economic sense."[8]

—Lee Crockett, director of Global Partnership for Sharks and Rays

But successes are not always easy or lasting. The mid-Atlantic summer flounder was overfished for decades. NOAA Fisheries began a recovery program, but the program only gave the flounder an 18 percent chance of avoiding overfishing. When more restrictive regulations were introduced, the recovery rate increased. The spawning stock had increased tenfold by 2010. But then, flounder production decreased sharply in 2010 and for the six years thereafter. No cause was determined. Because of the decreased stock, NOAA Fisheries recommended a 30 percent reduction in catch for 2016.[7] Fishers and politicians objected. According to a writer for the Ocean Conservancy, the fishing industry focuses on short-term impacts of reducing harvest, in part because of consumer demand, while fishery managers focus on the long-term health of the fish population. To maintain a healthy, sustainable fishery, the long-term approach is essential.

INVESTING IN FUTURE FISH

Investors are also setting their sights on the recovery of fisheries in the developing world. Chile's common hake fishery collapsed in the early 2000s. The Encourage Capital Fund plans to help the population grow. The recovery is expected to cost $20 to $40 million. As of 2016, the Sustainable Ocean Fund planned to invest $100 million in 10 to 15 fisheries in regions including Belize, Bangladesh, and Madagascar.[8] Both groups consider fisheries good investments. A study by two universities and the Environmental Defense Fund reported that in ten years, as much as 79 percent of the world's fisheries could be restored. This would lead to annual profits of about $51 billion. Improvements in fishery management would increase this profit over time. The strategy for recovering Chile's hake population, in addition to sending a lot more fish to market, would add $104 million in income for 1,800 fishers in 12 communities.[9]

Although many world fisheries are in dire straits, there is reason for optimism. The demand for seafood

SAYING NO TO SHARK-FIN SOUP

Shark finning is a cruel practice in which a shark's fins are cut off and the shark is returned to the water, often still alive. The shark cannot swim without its fins. It sinks to the bottom, where other fish eat it alive. Every year, as many as 73 million sharks are killed, some for their fins.[10] Claudia Li founded Shark Truth, which is now part of the Hua Foundation, in 2009. Li's goal was to save sharks traditionally killed for use in shark-fin soup for Chinese weddings. She asked wedding couples to remove shark-fin soup from their wedding menus. Those who did got the chance to win a free honeymoon to swim with sharks in Mexico. In three years, Li's contest stopped 80,000 bowls of shark-fin soup from being served and saved 8,000 sharks.[11]

means many people are committed to restoring and maintaining fisheries. The recognition of the importance of fish populations to marine ecosystems provides further motivation. Finally, the ability of many fish species to bounce back in approximately ten years means that success is nearly guaranteed, given a healthy environment and sustainable fishing.

The summer flounder lives on the ocean floor, burrowing into the ground to wait for prey.

MARINE BIODIVERSITY

Biodiversity, or biological diversity, is a measure of all the different kinds of organisms living in a specific area. Ocean biodiversity includes everything from gigantic blue whales to tiny single-celled algae. One form of biodiversity is species diversity, or the variety of species in an area. Species diversity is defined by two factors: the number of species present and the number of individuals of each species.

Ocean biodiversity is partially limited by sunlight, which penetrates only the top layer of ocean water, down to a depth of approximately 660 feet (200 m). Approximately 90 percent of all marine life exists in this layer.[12] Ocean life depends on photosynthesis by vast populations of tiny phytoplankton in offshore waters and by rooted plants near shore. These green organisms are at the bottom of most ocean food webs. In shallow water, photosynthesis supports both plankton and rooted plants, plus many benthic animals such as crabs, snails, and sea stars. Tropical coral reefs are the world's most biodiverse ecosystems. Other diverse tropical ecosystems include onshore mangrove swamps and underwater seagrass beds. In temperate zones, salt marshes flourish in the intertidal zone, while seagrass and kelp beds thrive offshore. Because of extreme cold and low light, polar biodiversity is much lower, but it includes many large animals, such as whales, seals, walruses, and polar bears. The least biodiverse region is the open ocean, where nutrients are scarce.

Ocean biodiversity provides humans with food, medicines, and oxygen. It detoxifies pollutants and recycles nutrients. Loss of biodiversity decreases the ecosystem's ability to function and survive. One of the greatest dangers to ocean ecosystems is declining biodiversity.

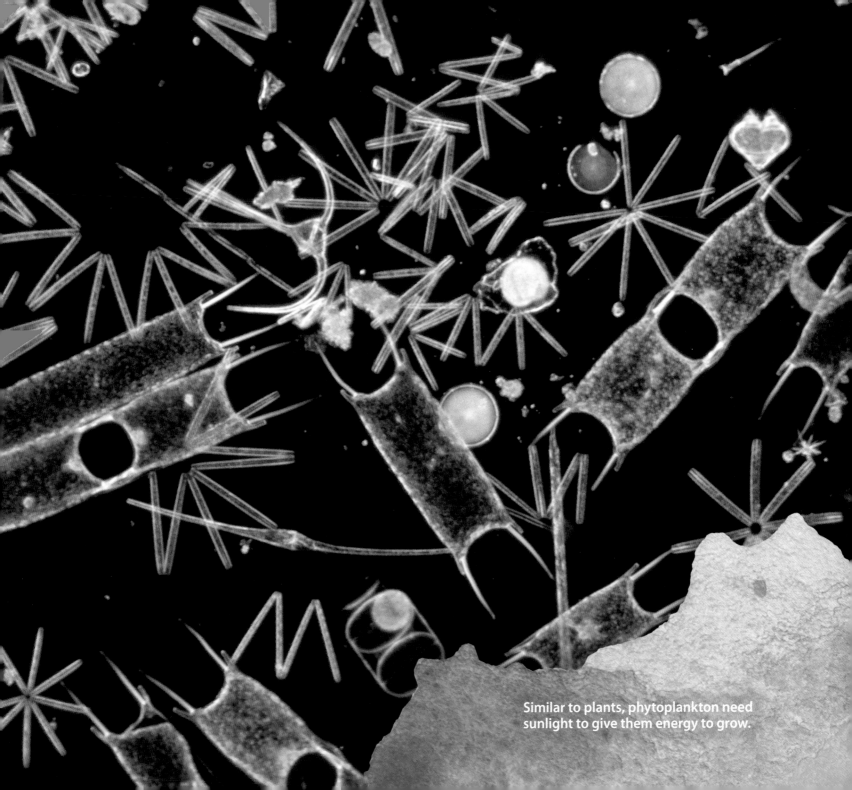

Similar to plants, phytoplankton need sunlight to give them energy to grow.

Shrimp trawlnets can catch many fish and other marine animals.

BYCATCH VERSUS BIODIVERSITY

M arine mammals such as whales, dolphins, and seals frequently become tangled and drown in fishing nets or trawls. They are also highly sensitive to sounds. NOAA researchers decided to try alerting marine mammals to the presence of fishing nets using acoustic pingers, or underwater sound-emitting devices. Pingers are set to a specific sound intensity and are attached to fishing gear, primarily gillnets. Researchers hoped if mammals heard the pingers, they would avoid the nets.

NOAA researchers studied the effectiveness of acoustic pingers in a California gillnet fishery between 1990 and 2009. They studied bycatch without pingers

Scientists believe that pingers encourage dolphins to echolocate. This helps them find the fishing gear and avoid swimming into it.

beginning in 1990. Pingers were added to the gillnets in 1996. This led to a 50 percent reduction in tangling of cetaceans, mostly common dolphins.[1] The number of pingers in a net varies according to net size and animals' swimming speed. Currently, three to four pingers are attached to a net 660 feet (200 m) long.[2] This works well for humpback whales and dolphins swimming at normal speeds, but it does not alert dolphins swimming rapidly and directly at the net. Pingers in the study seldom failed, but when more than one pinger in a net failed, ten times more dolphins became entangled. Although the pingers deterred most dolphins, they attracted California sea lions. Almost double the number of sea lions were caught in nets with pingers.[3] Researchers called this the "dinner bell" effect because the animals knew food was being gathered in the nets. Some fisheries in the US Northwest Atlantic, California, and Europe are now required to use acoustic pingers. Researchers hope to overcome the dinner-bell effect by changing the pinger's frequency so it is above the frequency sea lions can hear.

WHAT IS BYCATCH, AND WHY DOES IT MATTER?

Bycatch includes nontarget fish species, sea turtles, seabirds, and marine mammals such as seals, sea lions, whales, and dolphins. These animals become entangled in longlines, gillnets, or trawls. Turtles, seabirds, and mammals breathe air, and they drown when pulled underwater and trapped by nets or lines. Fishers typically target a single species, such as tuna or shrimp. But the target species does not live alone; it is part of a biodiverse ecosystem. It is nearly impossible to catch only that target species. The gear scoops up or hooks everything in the vicinity. In the Gulf of Mexico, shrimp are harvested in trawls dragged behind boats. Fishers may catch and throw out more than 6 pounds (2.7 kg) of bycatch for every pound (0.5 kg) of shrimp caught in a trawl.[4]

LIMITING UNSEEN BYCATCH

In Alaska's Bering Sea, the benthic ecosystem contains a rich mixture of groundfish and shellfish. Red king crab is often bycatch in groundfish trawls. Trawls consist of two long cables, or sweeps, which attach to the mouth of a net and pull the net forward, herding groundfish into it. But crabs cannot be herded; many are run over by the trawls and left to die on the bottom. To limit this "unseen bycatch," biologists devised a method to estimate crab death, then modified trawls to limit it. Modified trawls have rollers that raise the sweeps off the seafloor. The sweeps still herd groundfish, but they decrease king crab deaths by approximately 60 percent.[5]

Bycatch threatens the survival of species and ecosystems. In 2014, at least 7.3 million short tons (6.6 million metric tons) of marine organisms per year were caught as bycatch around the world. A few marine species risk extinction due to uncontrolled bycatch. The North Atlantic right whale has only 400 individuals remaining because of bycatch on fishing lines.[6] Bycatch threatens more than 15 percent of shark species with extinction.[7] It also kills young fish, which—had they survived—could have reproduced and rebuilt populations.

> "I care about bycatch because you can't just push a button and make more fish. So I make sure conservation is part of the experience. That means we don't take more fish than we need, and make sure the fish we release to swim away, don't float away."[10]
>
> —*Steve Witthuhn, captain, Top Hook Fishing Charters, New York*

More than 300,000 dolphins, porpoises, and small whales die every year as bycatch.[8] Entanglement in fishing nets is their largest cause of death. Several hundred thousand seabirds, approximately 200,000 loggerhead turtles, and 50,000 leatherbacks die annually as bycatch in gillnets, longlines, and trawls.[9] Bycatch is expensive and time-consuming for fishers as well. It damages fishing gear, and fishers must spend time separating bycatch from target species and throwing it back. The percentage of bycatch that dies after being thrown back is unknown, but it is thought to be high. Discards are greatest in trawl fisheries for shrimp and groundfish.

BETTER TECHNOLOGY DECREASES BYCATCH

Bycatch first became an issue for Americans in the 1960s with the deaths of dolphins in Pacific purse seines. These are nets that have floaters on the top end and weights on the bottom. They are drawn around a group of fish. In the eastern tropical Pacific, yellowfin tuna are often associated with dolphins. Fishers deploy a purse seine around the dolphins, capturing the tuna below them. They try to release dolphins from the top, but many become entangled and die. In the 1960s and 1970s, the death toll averaged approximately 500,000 dolphins every year. The 1972 Marine Mammal Protection Act included a requirement to decrease this number. By 1980, the US dolphin kill was reduced to approximately 20,000 dolphins per year.[11] Declines in dolphin deaths resulted from a combination of factors, including scientific studies, observers on fishing boats, inspection and modification of fishing gear, and better fishing procedures. Information from all of these factors led to new regulations to limit dolphin kills. The protections later became international, and US manufacturers introduced tuna branded as dolphin safe, or caught without setting nets around dolphins.

All types of fishing gear are nonselective. They will catch many other kinds of animals than the

RESCUING A TRAPPED WHALE

NOAA and other agencies maintain emergency response teams to disentangle whales from fishing gear. First, they attach a satellite transmitter to the entangling line. This allows them to track the whale so they can find it later. Then they attach an inflatable boat to the entangling lines. This slows the whale down, allowing rescuers to get close enough to work. In 2013, a response team in the Hawaiian Islands rescued an entangled humpback whale. On the first day, they cut away 40 feet (12 m) of line. Several days later, they located the whale using its satellite tracker and removed another 200 feet (60 m) of line, freeing it completely.[12]

Dolphin safe labels on tuna cans tell consumers the tuna was not caught with purse seines.

target species. Groups working to reduce bycatch want to modify gear so it catches fewer nontarget species or allows bycatch species to free themselves. The WWF sponsors the International Smart Gear Competition to encourage engineers to develop fishing gear that will decrease bycatch. The $50,000 in prize money, which has so far been awarded in 2011 and 2014, has resulted in gear that has reduced the bycatch of seabirds and sea turtles.[13]

Improved gear can be high-tech, such as TEDs that allow sea turtles and other large animals to escape nets or shrimp trawls. It can be low-tech, such as the inexpensive streamer lines used to scare seabirds away from longlines. Other changes do not involve gear modifications. Satellite tracking collects data on turtle migrations. This tells researchers where turtle feeding areas are, and it anticipates where turtles will come into contact with fisheries and fishing gear. Letting fishers know which areas to avoid can help prevent turtle losses. If an area has high concentrations of particularly vulnerable bycatch species, such as a critically endangered species, the area might simply be closed to fishing.

SOMETIMES CONSERVATION FAILS

Not all marine conservation stories are successes. The highly endangered vaquita is a tiny porpoise that lives only in the northern Gulf of California. It is the smallest and rarest of marine mammals. A 2016 survey estimated that vaquita numbers had decreased to only 30 individuals—half of its 2015 population, and

CIRCLE HOOKS SAVE LIVES

The typical hooks used in longline fishing are J-hooks. These cause suffocation or internal bleeding when sea turtles swallow them. The WWF is working with partners, including the Inter-American Tropical Tuna Commission, to replace J-hooks with circle hooks. When introduced into eastern Pacific longline fisheries, circle hooks reduced sea turtle deaths by 90 percent.[14] The WWF is now looking to expand the program. This would affect ships with longlines throughout Papua New Guinea and the Solomon Islands.

one-third of its 2014 population.[15] Vaquitas are caught and drowned in nets targeting the totoaba fish. The totoaba is overfished and is listed as endangered by both Mexico and the United States. Its bladders are delicacies in Asia and are traded illegally from Mexico through the United States to China.

In 2017, the WWF predicted that the vaquita could become extinct by 2018 unless bycatch was eliminated immediately. The only way to save it, according to the WWF, was to ban all fishing in vaquita habitat. The WWF was committed to working with the Mexican government to enact this ban. It partnered with the US government to stop shipments of totoaba products. It also wanted to work with fishing communities to find sustainable economic alternatives to totoaba fishing. Even if all this could be accomplished, the vaquita's outlook was bleak. "What's so devastating about the vaquita is that it could go extinct with the majority of the world having no idea this beautiful animal even existed," says Leigh Henry, WWF senior policy advisor. "But I refuse to give up hope. We'll fight on."[16]

Henry's "fight on" attitude is vital for marine conservationists trying to decrease bycatch. Fishing will continue, and bycatch will continue with it, because of the biodiversity of fishery habitats. Decreasing bycatch is a complex goal, and methods vary by species. It requires research and continuing trials. Some trials will be successful; some will not.

The vaquita is an example of how bycatch can drastically shrink species populations.

But every trial teaches conservationists more about how animals respond and which methods work best. Every interaction conservationists have with fishers and governments increases their understanding of bycatch, the devastation it causes, and the actions every group can take to reduce it.

"Wherever there is fishing, there is bycatch."[18]

—WWF article on bycatch

Eelgrass, an important fish habitat, filters polluted water and keeps shores from eroding.

FIVE

SAVING REEFS AND ESTUARIES

Seagrasses live in shallow, sunny waters from the tropics to the poles. They are not the same as seaweeds, which are algae. Seagrasses actually are grasses. They have roots, stems, and leaves; they produce flowers and seeds. Seagrasses form highly productive underwater meadows that support a diversity of marine animals. But like other coastal marine ecosystems, they face environmental threats.

The major seagrass along the US East Coast is eelgrass. It provides food, shelter, and nursery areas for organisms from blue crabs to bay scallops to fish. In the 1930s, disease destroyed 90 percent of East Coast eelgrass.[1] By the end of the century, populations along the southern coast of Virginia still had not returned

BUGS AND SLUGS
SAVE SEAGRASSES

Eelgrass, in the genus *Zostera*, forms teeming ecosystems on both coasts. The slow-growing grass is threatened by eutrophication. The excess nutrients cause algae to grow very rapidly and smother the eelgrass, preventing sunlight from reaching it. Eelgrass is protected by small grazers such as crustaceans, worms, snails, and slugs that graze on algae, keeping the eelgrass clean. Marine biologist Emmett Duffy led a large experiment called *Zostera* Experimental Network in which biologists in 15 sites around the world tested the effects of grazing on eelgrass beds. They showed that algal grazing by these small animals was crucial in keeping eelgrass healthy—more crucial than environmental factors such as temperature or salinity. Also, the more biodiverse the grazers were, the healthier they kept the eelgrass.

to normal. Dr. Robert Orth of the Virginia Institute of Marine Science (VIMS) developed new methods for reseeding eelgrass. From 1999 through 2010, people put Orth's methods to the test. VIMS, NOAA, the Nature Conservancy, and other groups, including many volunteers, collected and spread 37.8 million eelgrass seeds over 309 acres (125.1 ha) in four bays. By 2012, the seeds had sprouted into 4,200 acres (1,700 ha) of lush eelgrass meadows.[2] This is the world's largest seagrass restoration and a landmark in marine conservation.

THREATS TO REEFS AND ESTUARIES

Estuaries and bays have lower salinity than the open ocean. They support seagrass beds at all latitudes, and those in the tropics support coral reefs. Both estuaries and bays are threatened by inputs from land and nearshore activities. The list of human-caused threats is long. Coastal development often completely destroys habitats by dredging, draining, filling, and damming. In some areas, up to 60 percent of estuaries have been converted for agricultural use, filled to expand cities, or dredged to create shipping ports.[3] Remaining areas may be highly polluted by oil and toxic chemicals from industry and runoff, excess nutrients from sewage and agriculture, and pathogens such as bacteria and viruses. In addition, non-native or invasive species can kill or outcompete native species.

Similarly to estuaries, coral reefs are threatened by urban and agricultural runoff, coastal development, and toxic pollutants. Erosion causes sediment to wash over the reefs, smothering corals and depriving them of light and oxygen. But coral reefs have additional problems. Boats, anchors, and careless tourists damage and destroy corals. Tourists and poachers rob reefs of corals, fish, and other organisms. Local businesses sell corals as souvenirs. Corals are ripped from reefs and sold to construction companies for use as bricks, road fill, and cement for buildings. Local fishers destroy reefs by overfishing or fishing with dynamite or cyanide poison.

Coral reefs are extremely susceptible to climate change. Rising temperatures and acid levels are stressing reefs around the world. The symbiosis between corals and the tiny algae inside them breaks down. The algae are expelled and the coral turns white, a process called coral bleaching. The corals die

SUPER SUCKERS SAVE REEFS

Super suckers are just what they sound like—gigantic vacuum cleaners. The beautiful coral reefs of Kaneohe Bay off the island of Oahu, Hawaii, were being smothered by invasive algae introduced by coastal aquaculture. So the Nature Conservancy and its partners mounted giant vacuum cleaners on barges and used them to suck the thick mats of algae off the reefs. As of 2015, they had removed hundreds of thousands of pounds of algae from reefs.

unless water conditions improve and the algae can return. Warmer temperatures increase coral disease. Increased water acidity interferes with corals' ability to build the calcium skeletons that provide the reef's structure.

SAVING BAYS AND ESTUARIES

The National Estuarine Research Reserve System monitors and protects the health of more than 1 million acres (400,000 ha) of coastal estuaries. This partnership between NOAA and coastal states collects data showing how human activities affect estuaries. It has 26 sites that automatically collect data to monitor water quality.[4] This helps scientists better understand estuaries, detect pollution, and evaluate levels of recovery and restoration. NOAA's Office of Response & Restoration works with two other NOAA agencies to restore damaged estuaries around the country. They respond to many oil spills every year. Most famously, they responded to the 2010

Algae is what gives coral its color. Without algae, coral turns white.

QUILTS SAVE OYSTER REEFS

In the Indian River Lagoon at Florida's Cape Canaveral National Seashore, powerboat wakes knocked oysters loose, turning oyster reefs into barren islands. To restore the reefs, Dr. Linda Walter of the University of Central Florida developed oyster quilts composed of thousands of square mats, each with empty oyster shells attached so they cannot be knocked off. When a quilt was placed in the water, young oysters quickly colonized it and grew, renewing the reef. Anne Birch of the Nature Conservancy turned Walter's idea into a large-scale project. She worked with NOAA's Community Based Restoration Program, other partners, and thousands of volunteers. Between 2005 and 2012, oyster quilts restored 42 oyster reefs in the Indian River Lagoon.[5]

Deepwater Horizon spill in the Gulf of Mexico. They work from Alaska to Florida restoring rivers and coastal areas damaged by hazardous waste releases.

State and nongovernmental organizations also protect and restore estuaries. Ten conservation groups, collectively called Restore America's Estuaries, cooperate to restore coastal ecosystems, replant salt marshes, and restore shellfish habitats, among other projects. Some organizations focus on saving specific estuaries. The Chesapeake Bay Foundation (CBF) works on Chesapeake Bay, the largest estuary in the United States. The CBF works to clean and restore the bay, sponsors educational programs, and sometimes sues polluters. The Washington State Department of Ecology actively protects Puget Sound, the country's second-largest estuary. The state runs a long-term Toxics Cleanup Program (TCP) in Puget Sound. The Salmon Creek Estuary lost nearly all of its salmon population for 50 years because of toxic runoff from the lumber industry. After a TCP, the estuary again supports salmon, shellfish, and birds.

SAVING CORAL REEFS

Some of the world's worst coral reef devastation is in the Caribbean, just off US shores. Caribbean reefs began declining in the 1980s because of disease, climate change, overfishing, and the death of sea urchins that had controlled algal growth. Today, most Caribbean corals are gone, and major coral reef restoration initiatives are now underway. The Global Coral Restoration Project is a joint venture of SECORE International, the Nature Conservancy, and the California Academy of Sciences.

This project begins with coral spawning. Coral eggs and sperm are collected, fertilized in the lab, and then the baby corals are cared for until they are ready to be moved to the reef area, where they can settle onto a solid surface and attach. This process has the potential to produce millions of genetically diverse baby corals that can repopulate the reefs. Project members are doing research and initial trials in the Caribbean, and they hope to expand to the Pacific as soon as possible. They also teach others how to conduct the restoration work.

"Estuaries rank along with tropical rainforests and coral reefs as the world's most productive ecosystems, more productive than both the rivers and the ocean that influence them from either side."[6]

—J. Harvey, D. Coon, and J. Abouchar, in a 1998 Conservation Council of New Brunswick report

Many groups are restoring corals. Dr. Diego Lirman of the University of Miami heads projects in the Dominican Republic and Honduras restoring staghorn and elkhorn corals. These rapidly growing branching corals once formed the major structure of Caribbean reefs and provided most of the habitat for reef organisms. They covered vast areas of the Caribbean in thickets more than 3 feet (1 m) high. In the 2010s, only occasional scattered

Staghorn coral branches grow 4 to 8 inches (10 to 20 cm) longer each year.

corals remain, no more than 8 to 12 inches (20 to 31 cm) high.[7] Dr. Lirman's group removes small fragments from parent coral colonies, moves them to a nursery area, and attaches them to structures such as metal frames or cement blocks. Once attached, the fragments are nurtured and allowed to grow. Eventually they are returned to the wild to help reform the reef.

"People have asked me what it will cost to restore all the corals back to the way they remember. But I have to ask them, what will it cost if we don't do anything?"[8]

—*Dr. David Vaughan, executive director, Mote Marine Laboratory*

Dr. Nancy Knowlton of the Smithsonian Institution co-led the Census of Coral Reefs project, which tried to document the great biodiversity of coral reefs. Knowlton is extremely concerned about the dangers to coral reefs. While she approves of coral restoration, she points out that it is not a cure-all. She explains, "Restoration only works if you have fixed the problem that caused the corals to disappear in the first place. In many places, that is not happening."[9] Currently, Knowlton says, the most widespread problem facing coral biodiversity is overfishing, but that danger is being rapidly overtaken by climate change. She favors managing local stressors, including overfishing and pollution. This will increase corals' resilience, making them better able to withstand the growing stress of climate change. Marine protected areas will help protect reefs. If reefs are protected and their stressors eliminated or decreased, coral restoration projects can help them regrow.

BREAKTHROUGH IN REEF RESTORATION

At Mote Marine Laboratory in Sarasota, Florida, a team of researchers led by executive director Dr. David Vaughan, pictured, uses the technology of microfragmentation and fusion to restore reefs. This method speeds the growth of slow-growing reef-builders, such as brain and boulder corals. Researchers salvage many thousands of tiny pieces of coral from damaged reefs, bring them into the laboratory, and grow them rapidly and safely until they are big enough to transplant back to the reef. Their transplanted corals have been growing on the new reefs for years, and 90 percent of them survive. Vaughan says, "I can see, in just my lifetime, we will replant these reefs the way I remember them being."[10]

CURRENTS: MOVING THINGS AROUND

Ocean currents are movements of ocean water from one place to another. Wind primarily affects surface currents, which form complicated patterns that move ocean water thousands of miles. Currents move warm water from the equator toward the poles, and cold water from the poles to the equator. Surface currents occur in the upper 1,300 feet (400 m) of the ocean and move the upper 10 percent of ocean water.[11] They result from the friction of wind on the water and from the Coriolis force, which is caused by Earth's rotation. These forces move water in circular patterns, or gyres. Movement is also influenced by the shape of Earth's continents and ocean basins. Northern Hemisphere gyres move clockwise; Southern Hemisphere gyres move counterclockwise.

Deepwater currents are below 1,300 feet (400 m) and move 90 percent of ocean water.[12] They are caused by differences in water temperature and salinity. As warmer water rises near the poles, it forces cold surface water down. This cold water moves as an underwater river toward the equator, where it warms and begins to rise. These deep currents move heat around the ocean. Deepwater currents are much slower than surface currents, taking 35.3 cubic feet (1 cu m) of water approximately 1,000 years to complete its journey around Earth.[13] The same amount of water moving in a surface current travels tens to hundreds of times faster.[14] When cold currents travel to warm climates, and warm currents to cold climates, it keeps those areas from having extreme temperatures.

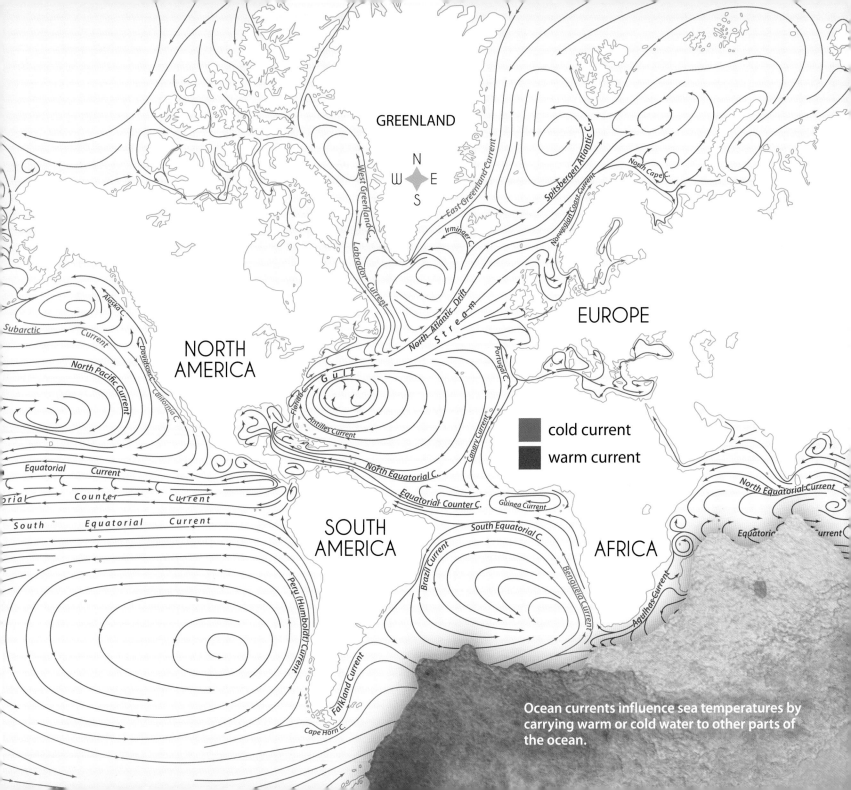

GREENLAND

N
W · E
S

EUROPE

NORTH
AMERICA

West Greenland C.

Labrador Current

East Greenland Current

Irminger C.

North Atlantic Drift

Spitsbergen Atlantic C.

Norwegian Coast Current

North Cape C.

Stream

Gulf

Florida C.

Antilles Current

North Equatorial C.

Portugal C.

Canary Current

Alaska C.

Subarctic   Current

Davidson C.   California C.

North Pacific Current

Equatorial   Current

Counter   Current

South   Equatorial   Current

SOUTH
AMERICA

Equatorial Counter C.

Guinea Current

South Equatorial C.

AFRICA

North Equatorial Current

Equatorial   Current

cold current

warm current

Peru (Humboldt) Current

Falkland Current

Cape Horn C.

Brazil Current

Benguela Current

Agulhas Current

Ocean currents influence sea temperatures by carrying warm or cold water to other parts of the ocean.

Plastic trash can get caught around marine animals and eventually kill them.

Chapter SIX

OCEAN POLLUTION

Plastic waste reaches every part of the ocean. But one pair of entrepreneurs decided it was an untapped resource too valuable to enter the ocean. They decided to use it to help solve another world problem—poverty. In 2013, David Katz and Shaun Frankson founded the company Plastic Bank. Plastic Bank is based on recycling. It gives people in poor communities an incentive to collect plastic waste before it enters the ocean. Local entrepreneurs operate convenience stores where the currency is plastic waste, or "social plastic." Anyone can collect plastics to provide for their family and send their children to school. They are paid in money or goods and services including wireless Internet access, sustainable cooking fuels, or electricity for charging mobile phones. The plastic is pelletized and sold to companies as raw material for manufacturing, such as for use in 3D printers or as packaging.

Plastic Bank has big plans. In 2015, they launched Plastic Bank in Haiti, using solar power for recycling. By 2017, they had expanded into the Philippines and were planning branches in Indonesia and Brazil. They are working with IBM to create a new digital currency and exchange system called Plastic Bank App that will take the operation worldwide. Through IBM, they will create a new software called Hyperledger Fabric. This will allow people, especially those in areas of poverty, to use plastic waste as currency. Plastic Bank may become a model for future solutions to ocean pollution. It won't run out of plastic anytime soon. Many other projects are underway to help solve the plastics problem.

People in many countries including Bangladesh can collect plastic debris and sell it or trade it for services.

THE PROBLEM OF OCEAN POLLUTION

Eighty percent of ocean pollution comes from land and seriously affects coastal areas.[1] Most of it is nonpoint source pollution, or general runoff from city streets, parking lots, lawns, septic tanks, vehicles, and farms. It includes oil, excess nutrients from fertilizer and sewage runoff, and air pollution that settles into the water. Some is topsoil from agriculture and construction sites. Point source pollution from identifiable locations adds to the problem. Often, these are massive oil spills from oil tankers or drilling rigs. Although less common, they have large, immediate impacts. All pollution damages ocean wildlife and habitats.

One of the largest and most publicized types of ocean pollution is plastic waste. Every year, 8.8 million short tons (8 million metric tons) of plastic waste enter the world's ocean with devastating effects to marine wildlife.[2] A 2015 study estimates that by 2020, ocean plastic input will increase tenfold.[3] Plastic is everywhere in human society, from plastic wrappers, bags, and bottles to disposable goods. Anything that enters a sewer system can eventually make it to the ocean. Discarded fishing nets and lines form a big part of ocean plastics. Plastics float on the surface and do not biodegrade, but wind and waves wear them down to tiny pieces, which

DO COASTAL CLEANUPS WORK?

The Ocean Conservancy's International Coastal Cleanup is dedicated to cleaning up the sea. In 2015, hundreds of thousands of volunteers collected millions of pounds of trash—much of it plastic—on beaches around the world. They removed plastic bottles, food wrappers, plastic bags, bottle caps, straws and stirrers, plastic lids, and the most common items: cigarette butts. Beach trash is a small part of the ocean pollution problem, but it is important. Trash removed from the beach no longer hurts beaches, marine animals, or local economies.

animals ingest. Larger pieces entangle ocean animals including whales, dolphins, seals, turtles, and seabirds. On Midway Atoll in the Pacific Ocean, 2,000 miles (3,000 km) from any continent, photographer Chris Jordan documented dead albatross chicks.[4] Their stomachs were filled with bottle caps, cigarette lighters, and other trash, fed to them by parents who mistook the floating plastic for food.

Plastics travel with ocean currents and eventually reach the gyres that form in all major oceans. The trash stays trapped in the calm centers of these gyres and extends throughout the water column. The Great Pacific Garbage Patch in the North Pacific Ocean is the largest, but every ocean gyre has one. North Atlantic currents now carry plastic trash even into the remote Arctic Ocean. Plastic debris does not form obvious islands of trash. Much of the pollution is like pepper in a soup, composed of tiny pieces, or microplastics, mixed with larger pieces, such as fishing gear, shoes, and Styrofoam cups.

COTTON TACKLES OIL SPILLS

Oil spill cleanup consists mostly of corralling the oil inside booms or dispersing it with toxic chemicals. Cotton may improve this situation. A type of low-quality cotton usually rejected for consumer use is especially good at soaking up oil. It is more useful than high-quality cotton, because its waxy coating absorbs oil but not water. One pound (0.5 kg) of the low-grade cotton absorbs 30 pounds (14 kg) of oil.[5] This cotton could help farmers by providing a market for otherwise unusable cotton, and it could help the ocean by cleaning up oil spills.

SOLUTIONS TO OCEAN POLLUTION

There are two basic solutions to all kinds of ocean pollution: stop it before it enters the ocean, or remove it after it gets there. Removing pollutants is impossible in many cases because the pollutant dissolves, becomes diluted, or covers too large an area. Stopping pollution before it enters the ocean also can be done in two ways: collect pollutants before they enter the ocean, or stop making the pollutants in the first place. In the case of plastics, both scientists and explorers agree the ultimate solution is transitioning to a world economy not based on disposable plastics—that is, to stop putting plastics into the environment. Some companies, with the encouragement of environmental organizations, are moving from toxic, disposable plastics to biodegradable or reusable materials.

Several companies such as Plastic Bank are recovering waste plastics and using them as raw materials. The cleaning company Method began by producing environmentally friendly cleaning products. In 2011, it added recovered ocean plastic to its recycled plastic by incorporating waste collected on Hawaiian beaches into new plastic containers. It hopes more and more recovered ocean plastic will be used in packaging. Singer Pharrell Williams champions clothing made from ocean plastics. He has partnered with G-Star Raw, Bionic Yarn, and Parley for the Oceans to develop a clothing line called Raw for the Oceans. Bionic Yarn turns shredded waste plastic into fibers to make denim for the line's jeans, jackets, and hoodies. Over three seasons, it used the equivalent of two million plastic containers recovered from ocean coastlines.[6]

Boyan Slat wants to remove the plastic already in the ocean. Slat founded the nonprofit Ocean Cleanup Foundation at age 18 in 2013 and is refining the design for his Ocean Cleanup Array. The network of floating booms, or temporary floating barriers that contain plastics, and processing platforms can be moved to different marine garbage patches around the world. The network is anchored and spans the radius of a garbage patch. The angled booms form a funnel that uses natural ocean currents to concentrate the plastic and move it toward the platforms. On the platforms, plastic is separated from plankton, filtered, and stored prior to recycling. The array began testing in 2016, and its final launch is expected in 2020. The company hopes it will eventually help clean up the Great Pacific Garbage Patch. However, marine scientists have many concerns about the project. Among other things, they worry about bycatch, including fish, plankton, and larger floating organisms such as jellyfish.

"The reality is that only by preventing synthetic debris—most of which is disposable plastic—from getting into the ocean in the first place will a measurable reduction in the ocean's plastic load be accomplished."[8]

—*Charles Moore, discoverer of the Great Pacific Garbage Patch*

People can slow the flow of plastics and other pollutants into the ocean. They can refuse to buy water in plastic bottles, boycott products containing tiny plastic beads called microbeads, and support plastic bag bans. They can buy nondisposable products and participate in beach cleanups. But manufacturers must make the big changes. They must become much more serious about recycling their own production waste and using recycled materials in production. They must collaborate and share solutions.

In May 2017, the Ocean Cleanup announced it expected its system to clean up half of the Great Pacific Garbage Patch in five years.

While managing and collecting waste before it enters the ocean is important, ultimately society must move to never throwing things out. All trash and pollution must be recycled or redirected to other uses. This requires a combination of manufacturer commitment, government leadership and legislation, and individual cooperation.

THE EDIBLE WATER BALL

Americans use 50 billion plastic water bottles every year, more than three-fourths of which they throw away. Many of these end up in the ocean. Skipping Rocks Lab of London, England, wants to make plastic bottles obsolete. Their solution is Ooho—an edible water ball made of plants and seaweed. The Ooho is cheaper to make than plastic, is odorless and tasteless, edible, and biodegrades in four to six weeks.[9] As of 2017, the company was concentrating on Ooho's potential to replace plastic water bottles. In the future, it expects this natural substance to revolutionize the entire packaging industry.

Junction I-225   1
Belleview Ave   1¼
Orchard Road   3

Car exhaust releases carbon dioxide into the air, contributing to climate change.

SEVEN

THE OCEAN AND CLIMATE CHANGE

Climate change is causing major impacts on the ocean, and, like pollution, it begins on land with human activities. The major activity causing rapid climate change is the release of climate-warming greenhouse gases, including carbon dioxide, methane, and others, into the atmosphere. Greenhouse gases absorb heat and keep it in the atmosphere, a process called the greenhouse effect. This keeps Earth warm and able to support life, and until the beginning of

TEMPERATURES KEEP RISING

Earth set air temperature records in 2014, 2015, and 2016, with each average global temperature blowing past the previous year's record. NOAA's Goddard Institute for Space Studies (GISS) measures average monthly world temperatures. Compared to the 1951–1980 average temperature, the 2014 GISS temperature was 1.58 degrees Fahrenheit (0.88°C) higher, 2015 was 1.76°F (0.98°C) higher, and 2016 was 2.23°F (1.24°C) higher.[1] This rise was much steeper than usual because of the periodic weather anomaly known as El Niño, which was active during 2015 and 2016. Sixteen of the hottest 17 years on record have now occurred since 2000.[2] After the 2014 record was announced, US climate scientists warned that ocean warming is now unstoppable at the surface and in the upper layers. Ocean temperatures and sea levels will continue to rise for centuries because of the heat already in the atmosphere.

the Industrial Revolution from the late 1800s to the 1900s, levels of greenhouse gases remained balanced. However, as people began burning fossil fuels, long-stored greenhouse gases were released into the atmosphere. This began a runaway greenhouse effect, in which greenhouse gas levels rise, absorbing more heat and causing Earth's average temperature to rise. Agriculture also contributes nitrous oxide from fertilizers and methane from livestock, both potent greenhouse gases. Deforestation raises greenhouse gas levels because the carbon dioxide once removed by photosynthesis and stored in trees now remains in the atmosphere. Because climate change initiated by global warming is a global problem, it must be handled globally by fixing the source of the problem. Only when greenhouse gas emissions are mitigated will climate change slow, eventually lessening climate-based stresses on the ocean.

HOW CLIMATE CHANGES THE OCEAN

The ocean is Earth's major defense against global warming. For the past 200-plus years, the ocean has absorbed the results of fossil fuel burning: one-third of the excess carbon dioxide and 90 percent of the extra heat produced by greenhouse gases.[3] This absorption keeps the atmosphere much cooler than it would be otherwise. This is a result of water's very high specific heat capacity, meaning water absorbs considerable heat before changing temperature. Ocean temperatures rise more slowly than air temperatures, but noticeable ocean warming now extends down to greater depths than scientists have ever observed before. Ocean surface temperatures are at their highest since record keeping began in the late 1800s. Warming water is less able to hold oxygen, and ocean oxygen levels have been dropping since the 1980s. Scientists say the drop is faster than expected based on temperature increases, probably because of changing ocean circulation. Lower oxygen stresses marine organisms.

Warming has also led to sea level rise because of two major factors: melting land ice and thermal expansion, or an increase in water volume as the water warms. From 1972 to 2008, melting ice caused approximately 52 percent of sea level rise, and

SAVING ORMOND BEACH

In 2013, the Coastal Conservancy and the Nature Conservancy began a wetland restoration project on Ormond Beach, California. By purchasing and restoring 900 acres (360 ha) of coastal land, they are giving the sandy beach, dune, and wetland ecosystems the space they need to migrate inland as sea level rises.[4] The project will preserve habitat for marine organisms, migratory birds, and nesting shorebirds. It will also protect humans, since wetland ecosystems and dunes naturally absorb water and energy from sea level rise and storm surges.

thermal expansion caused 38 percent. But the melting rate is increasing; since 2003, more than three-fourths of sea level rise has been due to ice melting. Even if greenhouse gas emissions had dropped to zero by 2016, average world sea level would still rise 1.2 to 2.6 feet (0.37 to 0.8 m) by 2100 because of heat already trapped in the atmosphere.[5] But the rise will be greater, because excess greenhouse gases are still being emitted. Sea level rise is flooding coastlines. Between 1996 and 2011, coastlines from New York to Florida lost land, and floods became more frequent. Coastal wetlands such as salt marshes are drowning as sea levels rise too fast to keep grass-blades above water. Rising water means that offshore ecosystems, such as coral reefs and seagrass beds, are deeper underwater and receive less light, so photosynthesis decreases.

Finally, carbon dioxide dissolving into the ocean is causing an increase in ocean acidity. Even small increases in acidity disrupt corals' ability to construct their calcium carbonate skeletons. This decreases habitat and makes it harder for reef organisms to find food. Acidification, or the process of acid levels rising, may affect shellfish, whose shells are made from calcium carbonate. It may affect other marine organisms by slowing growth rates or changing their functions, such as their ability to breathe and smell.

THE PARIS CLIMATE AGREEMENT

Solving a global problem such as climate change requires global cooperation. The United Nations (UN) Framework Convention on Climate Change finalized the Paris Agreement on December 12, 2015. This comprehensive global treaty involves countries around the world,

Environmentalists gathered near the Eiffel Tower in Paris, France, to voice their opinions during negotiations for the Paris Agreement.

both industrialized and developing. A total of 196 nations signed onto the agreement. Only two did not sign: Syria, which was in the midst of a civil war, and Nicaragua, which thought the treaty did not do enough to protect the climate. The goal of the Paris Agreement is to limit global warming to less than 3.6 degrees Fahrenheit (2°C), and to aim for a limit of 2.7 degrees Fahrenheit (1.5°C).[6] Meeting this goal requires limiting the total release of greenhouse gases. Progress will be monitored and new target goals set every five years. The Obama administration, represented by then secretary of state John Kerry, helped develop the agreement and signed it in April 2016. However, on June 1, 2017, US president Donald Trump said the United States would leave the Paris Agreement in 2020, saying it would harm US economic growth. All other countries pledged to continue their efforts to combat climate change, as did many US mayors, governors, and corporate leaders.

"Climate change represents humanity's first planetwide experiment."[7]

—*David Biello,* Scientific American's energy and environmental editor

The Paris Agreement requires all countries to lower their greenhouse gas emissions, but countries develop their own plans to achieve this. Climate experts, including those from the International Panel on Climate Change, define two general mechanisms for dealing with climate change: climate mitigation and climate adaptation. Mitigation involves permanently reducing or eliminating the main cause of climate change—excess greenhouse gas emissions. Adaptation involves adjustments enabling human or natural systems to live with the changing climate. The two mechanisms complement each other and must be used simultaneously. More mitigation will result in less need for adaptation.

ADAPTATION AND MITIGATION AT SEA

Given the accelerating rate of climate change, many marine organisms may not be able to adapt quickly enough to survive. Small changes in temperature and acidity can strongly affect organisms, especially those unable to move, such as corals. This makes mitigation even more essential. To preserve marine ecosystems, people can help marine organisms adapt to rising temperatures, sea levels, and acidity.

The Center for Ocean Solutions is working on adaptations to ensure the ocean can withstand climate change. This partnership of several organizations from Stanford University and the Monterey Bay Aquarium works toward solutions for sea level rise, ocean acidification, ecosystem shifts, and ocean hypoxia, or decreased oxygen content. They hope their projects will increase resiliency of both ecosystems and human communities. The Cumulative Impacts Challenge deals with stresses on ocean ecosystems caused by the interaction of many impacts including climate change, pollutants, and overfishing. It does research on the legal and scientific aspects of these impacts and shares its information with decision makers to provide a baseline for future actions.

Its Coastal Adaptations Projects provide information to coastal planners about the importance of maintaining natural, as opposed to built, coastal infrastructure to provide ecosystem services. Another of its projects, the Kelp Forest Array, is an ocean-based

platform for conducting research on local effects of climate change on underwater kelp forests. Still another, the Ocean Tipping Points project, brings the concept of tipping points to ocean management. A tipping point is the point at which a small change in a factor such as temperature or acidity causes a large, often abrupt, change in a system. This project is developing tools to help marine conservation managers anticipate and recover from climate-caused tipping points in the marine environment.

SWITCHING TO ALTERNATIVE ENERGY

The major approach to fighting climate change is phasing out fossil fuels and developing an economy based on alternative, renewable energy sources. These include solar, wind, and geothermal power. Countries around the world are transitioning from fossil fuels to renewable energy. Many innovations are occurring in the European Union (EU) because of its Renewable Energy Directive, which requires

The Monterey Bay Aquarium also works to protect sea life such as southern sea otters.

ALTERNATIVE VERSUS RENEWABLE ENERGY

Renewable energy is generated from natural processes. It is continuously replenished and can therefore never run out. Renewable sources include sunlight, wind, tides, geothermal heat, water, and various types of biomass. Biomass is plant matter such as wood or grass that is burned to generate electricity. It is renewable because plants can be regrown, but, as with fossil fuels, biomass puts greenhouse gases into the atmosphere. Alternative energy is a general term for any source of energy that doesn't come from fossil fuel.

all EU countries to use at least 20 percent renewable energy by 2020.[8] Each country develops its own plan to use the renewable energy sources most suited to its geography and culture.

Sweden generates 32 percent of its energy from biomass and another 32 percent from hydroelectric and nuclear power. Latvia, with its long coastline on the Baltic Sea, generates much of its power from wind and is building a complete network of electric car charging stations. Finland is concentrating on making biofuel, energy from materials such as wood and grain, and plans to phase out coal during the 2020s. Its goal is to use 50 percent renewable sources by 2020 and be fully renewable by 2050. Wind power produces 42 percent of Denmark's electrical power. By 2050, Denmark plans to be 100 percent renewable, using no fossil fuels at all.[9]

Alternative energy has always meant "alternative to fossil fuels." But that has changed in the past three years, says Michael Liebreich, founder and chair of Bloomberg New Energy Finance (BNEF), an organization that researches energy. Solar and wind energy are no longer alternative but mainstream, and their prices are rapidly falling.

From 1975 to 2015, solar energy costs in the United States declined by 150 times, and the number of installations increased by 115,000 times. Declines are continuing. In April 2016, the cheapest contract for solar electricity was 3.6 cents per kilowatt-hour; by April 2017, the price had fallen 25 percent to 2.7 cents per kilowatt-hour. The cheapest wind contract fell from 5.3 cents to 4.9 cents per kilowatt-hour in the same year. Liebreich thinks these record low prices will soon become the norm. The average price for electricity in US homes is 12 cents per kilowatt-hour.[10] If he is correct, this spells a gigantic win for controlling climate change, and in the process, saving the ocean.

COSTA RICA GOES RENEWABLE

In 2015, the small Central American country of Costa Rica generated 99 percent of its electricity from renewables; for 285 days, it ran on renewables alone. Approximately three-fourths of Costa Rica's energy generation is hydroelectric because of its high tropical rainfall and abundant river flow.[11] The rest is a mixture of wind, geothermal, solar, and biomass energy. Numbers were slightly down in 2016—renewables supplied 98.1 percent, and the country ran for 250 days on renewables alone.[12] Costa Rica still relies on oil for heating and transport.

Maria Damanaki, *center*, is a strong advocate for sustainable fishing.

Chapter
EIGHT

THERE'S STILL WORK TO BE DONE

Maria Damanaki is a marine conservationist who works for the Nature Conservancy as global managing director of oceans. In a 2016 paper, she outlines three emerging trends for the future of ocean conservation. The first is increased reliance on science and technology. Because ocean environments are so huge and so challenging to work in, Damanaki sees new technology as vital, especially for data collection, which can be used in conservation efforts. Second,

DEVELOPING A SEA ETHIC

In 1949, conservationist Aldo Leopold published a classic essay titled "Land Ethic." He called for people to accept moral responsibility for the land and to treat it with respect. Carl Safina of the Safina Center Institute feels we must develop a sea ethic that applies this attitude to the ocean. A sea ethic would recognize the ocean as vital to the existence of life, including people. It would lead to a sense of commitment and urgency to fix ocean-based problems, from overfishing to climate change. A sea ethic would require respect for the world ocean.

she sees more collaborations between stakeholders whose goals differ but who all want to preserve the ocean. She points to Florida's Miami-Dade County area, where rising sea levels and storm intensity already threaten coastal communities. Engineers, economists, and conservationists led by the Nature Conservancy are working together to incorporate mangroves and coral reefs into storm and flood protection programs.

Finally, because the ocean is vast and is not owned by any single country, its protection requires global cooperation. Government collaborations and UN projects are a good start, says Damanaki. But better laws and regulations, binding agreements, and protective measures such as more marine protected areas are needed to ensure future ocean protection.

USING SCIENCE AND TECHNOLOGY

The new field of resilience science is quickly becoming an important part of ocean conservation. Ocean ecosystems are affected by many interacting stressors, from overfishing to pollution to climate change. The goal of resilience science is to learn how ecosystems resist, recover from, or adapt to these stressors. Resilience science concentrates on understanding interactions between marine organisms and humans, maintaining marine biodiversity, and monitoring ocean processes such as phytoplankton production. Scientists can use this knowledge to help protect all ocean ecosystems. Resilience science is already being applied in marine ecosystems around the United States, most notably in Chesapeake Bay.

Technology is assisting in ocean protection as well, and it will be even more important in the future. In 2014, three organizations—Oceana, SkyTruth, and Google—launched Global Fishing Watch. This project uses satellite data to provide a global picture of ocean fishing activity. According to John Amos, founder and president of SkyTruth, "Fishermen can show how they are doing their part to fish sustainably, we can motivate citizens to watch the places they care about, and we can all work together to restore a thriving ocean."[1]

Since 2012, South African scientists have been using robotic gliders to study climate change in the Southern Ocean. This ocean absorbs 50 percent of all carbon dioxide absorbed by the world ocean and is extremely sensitive to climate change.[2] It is also the least studied part of the ocean. The Southern Ocean Carbon and Climate Observatory research team uses the gliders to study physical processes, such as ocean eddies and currents, in the upper ocean. They are studying how these factors affect carbon dioxide exchange between ocean and atmosphere, as well as the growth of phytoplankton. Combining data from the robots with satellite data and computer models gives scientists a much more accurate picture of changing ocean features.

OCEAN ROBOTICS

South Africa's robotic glider fleet consists of nine units. Four gliders ride surface waves, measuring physical factors such as carbon dioxide and acidity, and five gliders can dive to a depth of 0.6 miles (1 km), collecting data as they dive.[4] Gliders send their data to satellites, which transmit the data to scientists in Cape Town, South Africa. The data are stored, analyzed, and released to researchers around the world. In the future, the team plans to upgrade the fleet by adding new sensors and more gliders.

Another promising technology is DNA analysis, which can identify the species of shark in shark-fin soup or the home population of a slain endangered whale. This is possible because of a new genetic database containing short DNA sequences from many of the world's species. This International Barcode of Life (iBOL) project has so far catalogued more than five million samples representing 525,000 species and aims to collect all species.[3] When iBOL samples are compared with samples tested in the field, DNA detectives can track seafood samples or dead animals to their origin. This helps them crack down on illegal fish and wildlife harvests and on mislabeled fish sold in restaurants.

COOPERATING TO SAVE THE OCEAN

A new global movement is forming to protect the ocean from future exploitation. It involves ocean conservation organizations working with politicians, fishers, and local communities to develop economics-based proposals to protect ocean biodiversity. Public-private partnerships involve local governments or communities focusing on a specific issue, such as nearby fisheries or food security. Tying these proposals to nationally important issues makes it more likely that conservation issues will be taken seriously. The conservation organization works as a partner, helping local leadership apply conservation principles. The private sector, with government support, will be important in scaling up marine protection to global levels. Private companies are particularly interested in long-term conservation of resources that can be marketed, such as fish or minerals.

The Ocean Foundation is one conservation organization working on ocean protection. Its mission is "to support, strengthen, and promote those organizations dedicated to reversing the trend of destruction of ocean environments around the world."[5] It works with interested donors to increase funds available for research, consulting, conservation projects, and speakers on topics related to the ocean and coasts. From its founding in 2003 through 2016, the Ocean Foundation spent millions of dollars on marine conservation projects such as habitat protection, species protection, ocean research and conservation, and public education about the ocean. The foundation is continuing to grow, suggesting it will continue to be a force for sustaining the world ocean.

THE FUTURE OF SEAFOOD INVESTIGATION

Dr. Paul Hebert, scientific director of iBOL, looks forward to the near future, when handheld instruments will test DNA samples quickly in the field. All marine organisms leave some of their cells in seawater. Collecting and testing a water sample for this environmental DNA would reveal all species of marine organisms that have been in the water that day. Scientists will be able to track migrating animals, identify species in a marine reserve, estimate a species' abundance, and even test fishing nets to ensure no banned species are being caught. This developing technology will greatly simplify and speed up many techniques vital to marine conservation.

GLOBAL OCEAN GOVERNANCE

The United Nations will continue to be vital to ocean conservation. At a UN summit in September 2015, world leaders adopted a set of 17 global Sustainable Development Goals (SDGs). Cooperating countries agreed that these were the highest priority global goals that countries should work on through 2030. Countries agreed to establish their own frameworks to achieve the 17 SDGs, which range from ending poverty to working on solutions for climate change and environmental pollution. In one of these, SDG 14, nations pledged to "conserve and sustainably use the ocean, seas and marine resources for sustainable development."[6]

"What we must do is encourage a sea change in attitude, one that acknowledges we are a part of the living world, not apart from it."[8]

—Dr. Sylvia Earle, marine biologist

The first UN Ocean Conference, held June 5–9, 2017, in New York City, was the first UN meeting devoted exclusively to the ocean. Participants shared research information, and they proposed management solutions regarding the future of the oceans. They discussed methods for tackling ocean problems and strengthened partnerships for achieving various goals. A major outcome of the conference was a Call for Action, which confirmed participants' commitment to meeting SDG 14. According to Dr. Ellen K. Pikitch, a professor and the executive director of the Institute for Ocean Conservation Science at Stony Brook University, "The UN Ocean Conference was pivotal in moving the focus from describing problems to catalyzing action."[7]

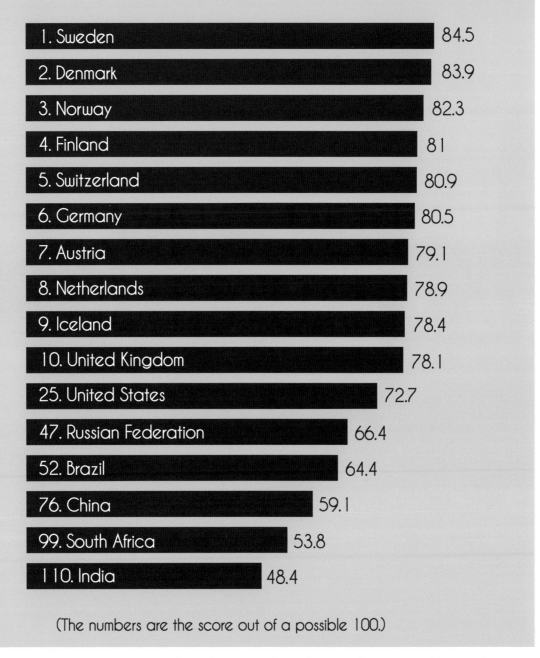

Rank	Country	Score
1.	Sweden	84.5
2.	Denmark	83.9
3.	Norway	82.3
4.	Finland	81
5.	Switzerland	80.9
6.	Germany	80.5
7.	Austria	79.1
8.	Netherlands	78.9
9.	Iceland	78.4
10.	United Kingdom	78.1
25.	United States	72.7
47.	Russian Federation	66.4
52.	Brazil	64.4
76.	China	59.1
99.	South Africa	53.8
110.	India	48.4

(The numbers are the score out of a possible 100.)

A 2016 study ranked countries in how they scored in achieving the Sustainable Development Goals. Results from criteria such as death rate and ocean biodiversity add up to the final score.

Channel Islands National Park in California has 13 MPAs.

At the UN Ocean Conference, governments, NGOs, foundations, businesses, and individuals made 1,393 voluntary commitments to ocean conservation; 28 percent of these commitments related to SDG target 14.5.[9] The target's goal was to use what scientists knew about the ocean to conserve 10 percent of ocean areas by 2020. Conserving marine areas by creating marine protected areas (MPAs) and seascapes has been one of the most successful forms of marine protection. An MPA is a region of ocean and any associated land that is internationally recognized and sustainably managed so that tourism, development, fishing, and other activities can continue indefinitely. A seascape is larger in scale. It is a multiple-use area managed by cooperating governments, businesses, communities, and other stakeholders. MPAs and seascapes are managed for the benefit of both ocean ecosystems and human well-being. The high proportion of commitments to MPAs at the UN conference indicates how important participants consider this form of ocean protection.

"In the end we will conserve only what we love; we will love only what we understand; and we will understand only what we are taught."[10]

—Baba Dioum, Senegalese forestry engineer and conservationist

The tiny island nation of Palau in the South Pacific is showing just how successful marine protected areas can be. In 2015, Palau designated an MPA area larger than California in which no fishing or mining could occur. Creation of the MPA was seen as essential to Palau's survival. The isolated island depends on the health of its fisheries and, as with other islands, is hard-hit by sea level rise and other impacts of climate change. After only two years, researchers found that the MPA had twice the biomass of fish and five times as many predatory fish as existed in unprotected waters.[11] These numbers indicate a healthy, thriving ecosystem. It also appears that the increase in fish reproduction will spill over into nonprotected areas, further improving the region's fish catch. According to Enric Sala, a National Geographic explorer-in-residence who worked on the Palau study, the success of the MPA resulted from local government policy combined with Palau inhabitants' strong culture of conservation.

The 10×20 Initiative, launched in October 2015 by the government of Italy and the Ocean Sanctuary Alliance, calls on each member-state to meet SDG target 14.5 by conserving 10 percent of its ocean area by 2020.[12] By November 2016, some nations (including Australia, Chile, Kiribati, Monaco, Palau, the United Kingdom, and the United States) had met their 10 percent targets, and other nations were near the goal.[13] However, US gains in marine protection under the Obama administration may be rolled back by the Trump administration. In an April 2017 executive order, Trump called for a review of large national monuments designated since 1996. He says protected lands and oceans jeopardize jobs and economic growth, and he wants them opened for oil and gas exploration. Some commercial fishers are also pushing to have them reopened for fishing. This executive order threatens five marine protected areas, including the world's largest marine national monument, in Hawaii. This change in policy illustrates that, no matter how hard ocean protectors work to save the oceans, the work is never done.

The ocean covers 71 percent of Earth's surface; thus, ocean problems are global and affect everyone.[15] Although the ocean continues to face a barrage of serious challenges, there is hope. Individuals, organizations, and governments around the world are concerned and are working together to find solutions. Support for MPAs is strong and growing. Ocean conservation groups have worked to replenish fisheries, minimize bycatch, restore reefs, clean up ocean plastics, halt coastal pollution, and address climate change. Projects in all areas are expanding. These efforts will have the best chance of success when people begin to treat the ocean not as a limitless dumping ground or a resource to exploit but as Earth's life-support system.

US MARINE PROTECTED AREAS

In 2015, the United States had more than 1,700 designated MPAs, covering 41 percent of its marine waters.[16] These areas have different uses and are not all equally protected. MPAs designed specifically to protect ocean biodiversity, ecosystems, and cultural resources account for only 8 percent of marine waters. Most MPAs are on the West Coast, but the region with the largest area covered is the Pacific Islands. This includes Hawaii's Papahānaumokuākea Marine National Monument, one of the world's largest marine conservation areas. Other protected areas are in the Gulf of Mexico and on the East Coast. However, as of April 2017, the Trump administration was reviewing five of these protected areas, totaling nearly 218 million acres (88.2 million ha), for possible removal from protected status.[17] Removing these areas from protection would open them to development, including oil and gas exploration.

CAUSE AND
EFFECT

Overfishing, illegal fishing, habitat destruction, and pollution cause fish catches to decline

Limit pollution

Close fisheries or set catch limits

Restore habitat or create MPAs and seascapes

Bycatch is a problem

Improve gear technology

Pass laws that limit bycatch

Pollution harms ocean ecosystems

Produce and release less plastic

Clean up pollution in ocean and along shore

Prevent release of toxins

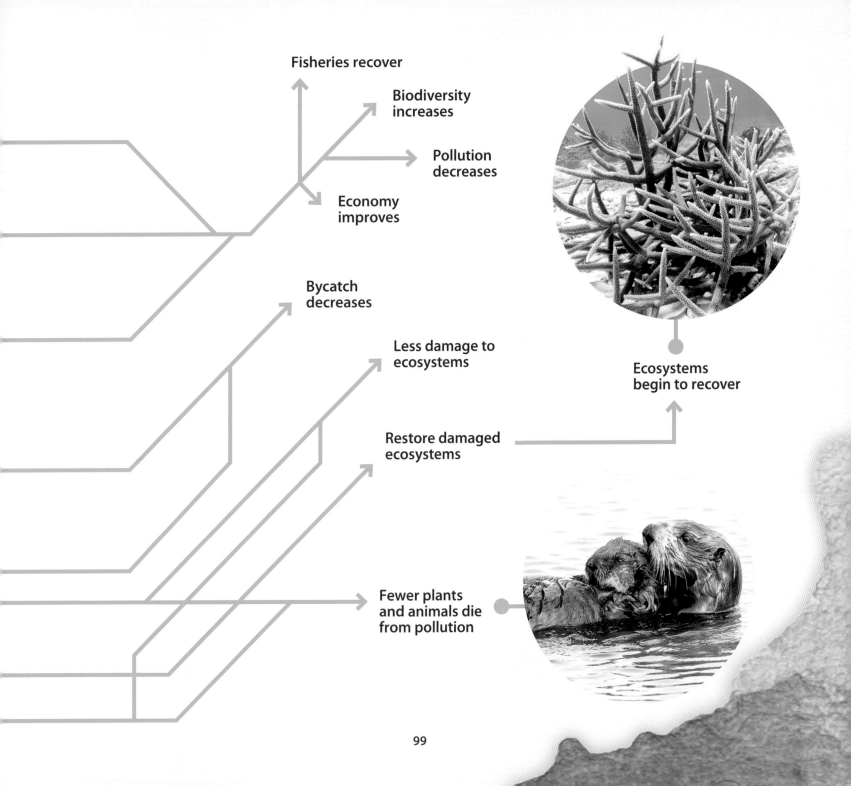

Fisheries recover

Biodiversity
increases

Pollution
decreases

Economy
improves

Bycatch
decreases

Less damage to
ecosystems

Restore damaged
ecosystems

Ecosystems
begin to recover

Fewer plants
and animals die
from pollution

ESSENTIAL
FACTS

WHAT IS HAPPENING

Ocean ecosystems are losing biodiversity, and habitats are being destroyed by overfishing, pollution, and climate change.

THE CAUSES

For centuries, people thought the ocean could provide an unending supply of resources and absorb and dilute any amount of pollution. But human populations exploded, rates of exploitation accelerated, and more and more waste was dumped into the ocean. In the last century, ocean fisheries have crashed, coastal ecosystems have been polluted or destroyed, plastics pollution has increased, and climate change has become a global threat.

KEY PLAYERS

- Marine conservation efforts are headed by university research organizations, nongovernmental organizations, and government agencies, such as NOAA Fisheries and the Office of Marine Conservation.

- Thousands of committed scientists are working on ocean problems. Charles Moore, Boyan Slat, the team of David Katz and Shaun Frankson, and Maria Damanaki of the Nature Conservancy are all working to restore the ocean.

WHAT IS BEING DONE TO FIX THE DAMAGE

Efforts are legal, governmental, and social, as well as science and technology based. Large-scale efforts often involve passing federal laws or intergovernmental agreements. A key protection is the designation of marine protected areas (MPAs) or seascapes. Scientists are adding to knowledge of the ocean and collecting data on subjects such as fish populations and plastic pollution. Data are used to enforce laws and regulations, as well as to develop plans for conservation and restoration. Governments, universities, and private organizations, usually aided by volunteers, are conducting restoration and cleanup projects on marine systems.

WHAT IT MEANS FOR THE FUTURE

Trends for future ocean conservation are continuations of current trends: more advanced science and technology, increased cooperation among governmental and nongovernmental groups, and increased global governance, including the establishment of marine protected areas. The most effective long-term conservation efforts will be those that prevent problems such as pollution or climate change.

QUOTE

"I look at marine conservation biologists as akin to the doctors of the ocean. And doctors don't train just to write obituaries. They fill medical journals with stories of advances and successes."

—*Dr. Nancy Knowlton, Smithsonian Institution*

GLOSSARY

AQUACULTURE

The process of raising fish and other aquatic animals for food.

BENTHIC

On or near the bottom of the ocean.

BOYCOTT

To refuse to have dealings with, usually in order to express disapproval or to force acceptance of certain conditions.

BYCATCH

The unintentional capture and sometimes subsequent death of nontarget animals during fishing.

ENTREPRENEUR

A person who organizes and operates a business or businesses.

ESTUARY

An area where river water meets seawater.

FISHERY

A fishing industry.

GILLNET

A flat net suspended vertically in the water so that a fish's head can pass through, but the net's mesh then traps fish by the gills if the fish tries to back out.

LONGLINE

A type of deep-sea fishing gear that may be many miles long with one long main line and shorter vertical lines with baited hooks attached at intervals where some are anchored and others are left to drift.

OUTCOMPETE

To outdo another organism in a competition for resources.

PHYTOPLANKTON

Tiny floating algae that form the base, or first level, of most ocean food webs.

RESILIENCE

The ability of an ecosystem or living thing to respond to a disturbance by resisting damage and recovering quickly.

SUSTAINABLE

In ecological terms, a population is sustainable if it can maintain its numbers under the conditions to which it is exposed; for example, a sustainable fishery can be harvested at a reasonable rate and not become depleted.

TRAWL

A large net dragged along the sea bottom.

WORLD OCEAN

The entire ocean, comprising approximately 71 percent of Earth's surface and including the five major oceans: Atlantic, Pacific, Indian, Arctic, and Southern.

ADDITIONAL RESOURCES

SELECTED BIBLIOGRAPHY

Damanaki, Maria. "What's the Future of Ocean Conservation?" *Nature Conservancy*. Nature Conservancy, June 2016. Web. 19 May 2017.

Malmquist, David. "Eelgrass Restoration Aids Overall Recovery of Coastal Bays." *VIMS*. VIMS, 20 Feb. 2012. Web. 19 May 2017.

Nature Conservancy. "Restoration Works: Coral Reef Restoration." *Nature Conservancy*. Nature Conservancy, 2017. Web. 19 May 2017.

Ocean Portal. "Success Stories in Ocean Conservation." *Ocean Portal*. Smithsonian National Museum of Natural History, 2016. Web. 19 May 2017.

Secretariat of the Global Ocean Commission. "Ocean SDG: Just a Big Splash, or a Genuine Sea Change?" *Future Oceans*. Future Oceans, 17 Feb. 2016. Web. 19 May 2017.

FURTHER READINGS

Dembicki, Matt. *Wild Ocean: Sharks, Whales, Rays, and Other Endangered Sea Creatures*. Golden, CO: Fulcrum, 2014. Print.

Hand, Carol. *Melting Arctic Ice*. Minneapolis, MN: Abdo, 2017. Print.

Perdew, Laura. *The Great Pacific Garbage Patch*. Minneapolis, MN: Abdo, 2017. Print.

ONLINE RESOURCES

To learn more about ocean conservation, visit **abdobooklinks.com**. These links are routinely monitored and updated to provide the most current information available.

MORE INFORMATION

For more information on this subject, contact or visit the following organizations:

Marine Conservation Institute

5010 Stone Way N, Suite 410
Seattle, WA 98103
206-547-1343
marine-conservation.org

This group works with governments and other groups to identify valuable ocean ecosystems and seek protected status for them.

National Oceanic and Atmospheric Administration (NOAA)

1401 Constitution Avenue NW, Room 5128
Washington, DC 20230
noaa.gov

NOAA is an agency of the federal government that uses science to collect data and provide citizens and decision makers with reliable information on climate, weather, the ocean, and coasts.

SOURCE NOTES

CHAPTER 1. SEA TURTLES: AN EARLY WARNING

1. "Multi-Species Recovery Plan for South Florida: Green Sea Turtle." *South Florida Listed Species*. USFWS: South Florida Ecological Services Field Office, n.d. PDF. 30 Aug. 2017.

2. "Green Sea Turtles Break Nesting Record on Florida Beaches." *Colleges & Campus News*. University of Central Florida, 2 Sept. 2015. Web. 30 Aug. 2017.

3. Rachel Nuwer. "Ultraviolet Illumination Warns Sea Turtles away from Fishing Nets." *Scientific American*. Scientific American, 1 Nov. 2013. Web. 30 Aug. 2017.

4. "Information about Sea Turtles: Threats to Sea Turtles." *Sea Turtle Conservancy*. Sea Turtle Conservancy, 2017. Web. 30 Aug. 2017.

5. Jennifer Kennedy. "10 Fascinating Facts about Sea Turtles." *ThoughtCo*. ThoughtCo., 20 June 2017. Web. 30 Aug. 2017.

6. Laura Sinpetru. "How Sea Shepherd Volunteers Helped Save 3,600 Baby Turtles." *SoftPedia News*. SoftPedia, 24 Oct. 2014. Web. 30 Aug. 2017.

7. "And the Winner of the 2016 Tour de Turtles Is . . ." *Sea Turtle Conservancy*. Sea Turtle Conservancy, 14 Nov. 2016. Web. 30 Aug. 2017.

8. Victoria Brook Van Meter. "Florida's Sea Turtles." Miami, FL: Florida Power & Light Company, 2002. 36. *Beaches Sea Turtle Patrol*. Web. 30 Aug. 2017.

9. "Interesting Ocean Facts." *SavetheSea.org*. SavetheSea.org, 2015. Web. 30 Aug. 2017.

10. "The Ocean Biome." *Windows to the Universe*. National Earth Science Teachers Association, 1 June 2010. Web. 30 Aug. 2017.

11. "Temperature of Ocean Water." *Windows to the Universe*. National Earth Science Teachers Association, 13 Feb. 2011. Web. 30 Aug. 2017.

12. Ibid.

CHAPTER 2. THE SCOPE OF MARINE CONSERVATION

1. "Threats to Oceans and Coasts." *WWF Global*. WWF for Nature, 2017. Web. 30 Aug. 2017.

2. Hélène Petit. "Open Ocean: Importance." *WWF Global*. WWF for Nature, 2017. Web. 30 Aug. 2017.

3. "#KnowYourOcean." *Woods Hole Oceanographic Institution*. Woods Hole Oceanographic Institution, 2017. Web. 30 Aug. 2017.

4. "Protecting Our Oceans." *Greenpeace*. Greenpeace, n.d. Web. 30 Aug. 2017.

5. Holly P. Jones and Oswald J. Schmitz. "Rapid Recovery of Damaged Ecosystems." *PLoS ONE* 4.5 (May 2009). *PLoS ONE*. Web. 30 Aug. 2017.

6. Rachel Dearborn. "Hey, Environmentalists, Let's Tell a Positive Story." *Medium*. Medium, 9 June 2014. Web. 30 Aug. 2017.

7. Nancy Knowlton. "Why Do We Have Trouble Talking About Success in Ocean Conservation?" *Smithsonian*. Smithsonian, 12 June 2014. 30 Aug. 2017.

8. "#KnowYourOcean." *Woods Hole Oceanographic Institution*. Woods Hole Oceanographic Institution, 2017. Web. 30 Aug. 2017.

9. Kieran Mulvaney. "Pathways to Ocean Success Stories." *Seeker*. Group Nine, 16 May 2011. Web. 30 Aug. 2017.

CHAPTER 3. SAVING OCEAN FISHERIES

1. Brett Bundale. "Haddock Stocks in Full Recovery." *Herald Business*. Chronicle Herald, 22 Jan. 2014. Web. 30 Aug. 2017.

2. "Big-Fish Stocks Fall 90 Percent Since 1950, Study Says." *National Geographic News*. National Geographic, 15 May 2003. Web. 30 Aug. 2017.

3. Gaia Vince. "How the World's Oceans Could Be Running Out of Fish." *BBC Future*. BBC, 21 Sept. 2012. Web. 30 Aug. 2017.

4. "Big-Fish Stocks Fall 90 Percent Since 1950, Study Says." *National Geographic News*. National Geographic, 15 May 2003. Web. 30 Aug. 2017.

5. Ibid.

6. Jay Odell. "Some Good Blue News: Ocean Success Stories." *Talk*. Nature Conservancy, 5 June 2009. Web. 30 Aug. 2017.

7. Charles A. Witek III. "It's Time to Do the Right Thing for Summer Flounder." *Ocean Conservancy*. Ocean Conservancy, 10 Mar. 2017.

8. "Success Story: Rebuilding America's Fisheries With One Single Act." *Pew Charitable Trusts*. Pew Charitable Trusts, 7 Apr. 2011. Web. 30 Aug. 2017.

9. David Bank. "Is the Recovery of Wild Fisheries the New J-Curve for Impact Investors?" *Impact Alpha*. Impact Alpha, 28 Jan. 2016. Web. 30 Aug. 2017.

10. "Ellen K. Pikitch." *Stony Brook University School of Marine and Atmospheric Sciences*. School of Marine and Atmospheric Sciences, 2017. Web. 30 Aug. 2017.

11. "Success Stories in Ocean Conservation." *Ocean Portal*. Ocean Portal, 2016. Web. 30 Aug. 2017.

12. "The Ocean Biome." *Windows to the Universe*. National Earth Science Teachers Association, 1 June 2010. Web. 30 Aug. 2017.

CHAPTER 4. BYCATCH VERSUS BIODIVERSITY

1. J. V. Carretta and J. Barlow. "Long-Term Effectiveness, Failure Rates, and 'Dinner-Bell' Properties of Acoustic Pingers in a Gillnet Fishery." *Marine Technology Society Journal* 45.5 (2011): 7–9. *Consortium for Wildlife Bycatch Reduction*. Web. 30 Aug. 2017.

2. C. Erbe, C. McPherson and A. Craven. "Acoustic Investigation of Bycatch Mitigation Pingers." *JASCO Applied Sciences* Report No. P001115-001-2 (7 Jul. 2011). *Consortium for Wildlife Bycatch Reduction*. Web. 30 Aug. 2017.

3. J. V. Carretta and J. Barlow. "Long-Term Effectiveness, Failure Rates, and 'Dinner-Bell' Properties of Acoustic Pingers in a Gillnet Fishery." *Marine Technology Society Journal* 45.5 (2011): 7–9. *Consortium for Wildlife Bycatch Reduction*. Web. 30 Aug. 2017.

4. "Wild Seafood: Bycatch." *Seafood Watch*. Monterey Bay Aquarium Foundation, 2017. Web. 30 Aug. 2017.

5. "The Bycatch You Can't See." *NOAA Fisheries*. NOAA Fisheries, n.d. Web. 30 Aug. 2017.

6. "What Is Bycatch?" *Consortium for Wildlife Bycatch Reduction*. Consortium for Wildlife Bycatch Reduction, 2014. Web. 30 Aug. 2017.

7. "Wild Seafood: Bycatch." *Seafood Watch*. Monterey Bay Aquarium Foundation, 2017. Web. 30 Aug. 2017.

8. "Bycatch." *WWF*. WWF, 2017. Web. 30 Aug. 2017.

9. "Wild Seafood: Bycatch." *Seafood Watch*. Monterey Bay Aquarium Foundation, 2017. Web. 30 Aug. 2017.

10. "Bycatch Bites." *NOAA Fisheries*. NOAA Fisheries, n.d. Web. 30 Aug. 2017.

11. "The Tuna-Dolphin Issue." *NOAA Fisheries*. NOAA Fisheries, 2 Sept. 2016. Web. 30 Aug. 2017.

12. Noah Press. "How to Disentangle a Tangled Up Whale." *NOAA Fisheries*, NOAA Fisheries, 29 Mar. 2014. Web. 30 Aug. 2014.

13. "International Smart Gear Competition." *WWF*. WWF, 2017. Web. 30 Aug. 2017.

14. "Bycatch." *WWF*. WWF, 2017. Web. 30 Aug. 2017.

15. "Vaquita Population Drops to 30 Individuals." *WWF*. WWF, 3 Feb. 2017. Web. 30 Aug. 2017.

16. Ibid.

17. "Bycatch Bites." *NOAA Fisheries*. NOAA Fisheries, n.d. Web. 30 Aug. 2017.

18. "Bycatch." *WWF*. WWF, 2017. Web. 30 Aug. 2017.

CHAPTER 5. SAVING REEFS AND ESTUARIES

1. Pamela L. Reynolds. "Seagrass and Seagrass Beds." *Ocean Portal*. Smithsonian, 2016. Web. 30 Aug. 2017.

SOURCE
NOTES *CONTINUED*

2. David Malmquist. "Eelgrass Restoration Aids Overall Recovery of Coastal Bays." *VIMS*. VIMS, 20 Feb. 2012. Web. 30 Aug. 2017.

3. "Human Disturbances to Estuaries." *NOAA Ocean Service*. NOAA, 6 July 2017. Web. 30 Aug. 2017.

4. "Monitoring Estuaries." *NOAA Ocean Service*. NOAA, 6 July 2017. Web. 30 Aug. 2017.

5. Judy Althaus. "Florida Oyster Reef Restoration." *Nature Conservancy*. Nature Conservancy, 2017. Web. 30 Aug. 2017.

6. J. Harvey, D. Coon, and J. Abouchar. "Habitat Lost: Taking the Pulse of Estuaries in the Canadian Gulf of Maine." Fredericton, NB: Conservation Council of New Brunswick, 1998. *Elements*. Web. 28 Aug. 2017.

7. Leaf Litter. "Thoughts on Coral Reef Restoration." *BioHabitats*. BioHabitats, 2017. Web. 30 Aug. 2017.

8. Julia Travers. "Mote Tropical Research Laboratory Works to Restore Florida's Coral Reefs." *Medium*. Invironment, 19 Apr. 2017. Web. 30 Aug. 2017.

9. Leaf Litter. "Thoughts on Coral Reef Restoration." *BioHabitats*. BioHabitats, 2017. Web. 30 Aug. 2017.

10. "Coral Reef Restoration." *Mote*. Mote Marine Laboratory & Aquarium, n.d. Web. 30 Aug. 2017.

11. Amanda Briney. "Ocean Currents." *ThoughtCo*. ThoughtCo., 3 Mar. 2017. Web. 30 Aug. 2017.

12. Ibid.

13. "Ocean Currents." *NOAA*. Department of Commerce, n.d. Web. 30 Aug. 2017.

14. "Currents: the Global Conveyor Belt." *NOAA Ocean Service*. NOAA, 6 July 2017. Web. 30 Aug. 2017.

CHAPTER 6. OCEAN POLLUTION

1. "What Is the Biggest Source of Pollution in the Ocean?" *NOAA Ocean Service*. NOAA, 6 July 2017. Web. 30 Aug. 2017.

2. Malorie Macklin. "3 Companies That Are Turning Ocean Plastic Pollution from a Problem to an Opportunity." *One Green Planet*. One Green Planet, 11 Nov. 2015. Web. 30 Aug. 2017.

3. Steve Conner. "Plastic Waste in Ocean to Increase Tenfold by 2020." *Independent*. Independent, 12 Feb. 2015. Web. 30 Aug. 2017.

4. Vanessa Carr. "An Ocean of Plastic." *PBS*. WNET.org, 9 Aug. 2010. Web. 30 Aug. 2017.

5. Kevin Mathews. "A New Solution for Oil Spills? You're Wearing It!" *Care2*. Care2, 20 May 2013. Web. 30 Aug. 2017.

6. Lorraine Chow. "Pharrell Williams and G-Star RAW Transform Ocean Plastic into Clothes." *EcoWatch*. EcoWatch, 19 Aug. 2015. Web. 30 Aug. 2017.

7. Nell Greenberg. "Captain Charles Moore . . . Talks Trash." *Earth Island*. Earth Island Journal, n.d. Web. 30 Aug. 2017.

8. Charles J. Moore. "Choking the Oceans with Plastic." *New York Times*. New York Times, 25 Aug. 2014. Web. 30 Aug. 2017.

9. Dylan Heyden. "Is this Edible Water Ball the Solution to Plastic Pollution?" *Inertia*. Inertia, 12 Apr. 2017. Web. 30 Aug. 2017.

CHAPTER 7. THE OCEAN AND CLIMATE CHANGE

1. "GLOBAL Station Temperature Index in 0.01 Degrees Celsius Base Period: 1951–1980." *Goddard Institute for Space Studies*. NASA, n.d. Web. 30 Aug. 2017.

2. Justin Gillis. "Earth Sets a Temperature Record for the Third Straight Year." *New York Times*. New York Times, 18 Jan. 2017. Web. 30 Aug. 2017.

3. "How Climate Change Relates to Oceans." *WWF*. WWF, 2017. Web. 30 Aug. 2017.

4. "Climate Change Success Stories: Ormond Beach, CA." *Explore Beaches*. Regents of the University of California, 2017. Web. 11 Sept. 2017.

5. "Causes of Sea Level Rise: What the Science Tells Us (2013)." *Union of Concerned Scientists*. Union of Concerned Scientists, 2015. Web. 30 Aug. 2017.

6. Emil Jeyaratnam, et al. "Paris Climate Agreement at a Glance." *Descrier*. Descrier, 14 Dec. 2015. Web. 30 Aug. 2017.

7. David Biello. "10 Solutions for Climate Change." *Scientific American*. Scientific American, 26 Nov. 2007. Web. 30 Aug. 2017.

8. Jess Tabinor. "The Innovative Use of Alternative Energy Across Europe." *Fircroft*. Fircroft, 19 Apr. 2017. Web. 30 Aug. 2017.

9. Ibid.

10. Joe Romm. "WATCH: Almost Everything You Know about Clean Energy Is Outdated." *Think Progress*. Think Progress, 4 May 2017. Web. 30 Aug. 2017.

11. AFP. "Costa Rica Boasts 99% Renewable Energy in 2015." *Yahoo News*. Yahoo News, 18 Dec. 2015. Web. 30 Aug. 2017.

12. Diana A.N. "For More than 250 Days of 2016, Costa Rica Ran Entirely on Renewables." *PVBuzz*. PVBuzz-Media, 6 May 2017. Web. 30 Aug. 2017.

CHAPTER 8. THERE'S STILL WORK TO BE DONE

1. "SkyTruth, Oceana & Google Announce New Technology Initiative to Illuminate Global Fishing Activity." *Oceana*. Oceana, 13 Nov. 2014. Web. 30 Aug. 2017.

2. Munyaradzi Makoni. "Robots Tell the Story of Climate Change in the Southern Ocean." *Future Oceans*. Future Oceans, 20 Jan. 2016. Web. 30 Aug. 2017.

3. Kenneth R. Weiss. "Seafood CSI: Advances in Genetic Technology Will Make Us All DNA Detectives." *Future Oceans*. Future Oceans, 9 Feb. 2016. Web. 30 Aug. 2017.

4. Munyaradzi Makoni. "Robots Tell the Story of Climate Change in the Southern Ocean." *Future Oceans*. Future Oceans, 20 Jan. 2016. Web. 30 Aug. 2017.

5. "About Us." *Ocean Foundation*. Ocean Foundation, n.d. Web. 30 Aug. 2017.

6. Secretariat of the Global Ocean Commission. "Ocean SDG: Just a Big Splash, or a Genuine Sea Change?" *Future Oceans*. Future Oceans, 17 Feb. 2016. Web. 30 Aug. 2017.

7. Ellen K. Pikitch. Email interview. 8 July 2017.

8. "A Sea Ethic." *Marine Bio*. Marine Bio, 2017. Web. 30 Aug. 2017.

9. Ellen K. Pikitch. Email interview. 8 July 2017.

10. Jennifer Kennedy. "What Is Marine Conservation?" *ThoughtCo*. ThoughtCo., 14 Dec. 2015. Web. 30 Aug. 2017.

11. Sarah Gibbens. "This Small Island Nation Makes a Big Case for Protecting Our Oceans." *National Geographic*. National Geographic, 3 Apr. 2017. Web. 11 Sept. 2017.

12. "10X20 Initiative." *Ocean Sanctuary Alliance*. Ocean Sanctuary Alliance, n.d. Web. 11 Sept. 2017.

13. Lance Morgan. "Progress Report on 10x20 Initiative." *Marine Conservation Institute*. Marine Conservation Institute, Nov. 2016. PDF. 11 Sept. 2017.

14. Ellen K. Pikitch. Email Interview. 8 July 2017.

15. "Aqua Facts." *Oceanic Institute*. Hawaii Pacific University Oceanic Institute, n.d. Web. 11 Sept. 2017.

16. "What Percentage of Marine Areas Are Protected?" *NOAA*. NOAA, 6 July 2017. Web. 11 Sept. 2017.

17. "Interior Department Releases List of Monuments Under Review, Announces First-Ever Formal Public Comment Period for Antiquities Act Monuments." *Press Releases*. US Department of the Interior, 5 May 2017. Web. 11 Sept. 2017.

INDEX

ABOUT THE AUTHOR

Carol Hand has a PhD in zoology with a specialization in marine ecology and a special interest in environmental and climate science. Her PhD dissertation was on coral reef fisheries. Before becoming a science writer, she taught college, wrote for standardized testing companies, and developed multimedia science curricula. She has written more than 40 books for young people, including many on science and environmental topics.